DATE DUE			
Nov 6 74			
Dec 11 74			
GAYLORD M-2			PRINTED IN U.S.A.

To

THE HON. HUGH McCULLOCH,

Secretary of the Treasury,

WHO FIRST

Of all our Northern Public Men

HAS HAD THE WISDOM, MAGNANIMITY, AND COURAGE

To express Sympathy for the Misfortunes

OF

THE SUBJECT OF OUR MEMOIR,

BY

A Visit to Mr. Davis in his cell at Fortress Monroe,

THIS VOLUME IS INSCRIBED.

PREFACE.

Owing to many inquiries and a demand created by the recent controversy, it is found expedient to republish a new edition of my father's book.

The facts contained in his work were carefully recorded and preserved by him while Chief Medical Officer at Fortress Monroe and published in 1866. It is hardly necessary to say that the incidents related by the author were then recognized as authentic. As a matter of history, this edition is now graciously offered to a new generation of readers.

WILLIAM DARCY CRAVEN.

EAST ORANGE, N. J.,
   Feb. 27th, 1905.

CONTENTS.

CHAPTER I.

PAGE

An Introduction by Ancodote.—The Old-fashioned
Preface in a New Dress 13

CHAPTER II.

Fortress Monroe.—The Ceremonial of delivering Mr.
Davis into Custody.—His first Day in the Casemate 22

CHAPTER III.

Placing Mr. Davis in Irons.—His Protest and his Struggles.—My First Visit to the Prisoner . . . 33

CHAPTER IV.

Conversation with Mr. Davis on many Points.—The
Removal of his Shackles demanded as a Medical
Necessity 44

CHAPTER V.

Conversations of some Interest.—The Shackles Removed.—Mr. Davis on Various Scientific Subjects 56

CHAPTER VI.

Operations on the Southern Coast.—Davis Hears that
he is Indicted and to be Tried.—His Joy.—Views
of his own Defence 70

CHAPTER VII.

Mr. Davis on the New England Character.—Future of
the South and Southern Blacks 84

Contents

CHAPTER VIII.

PAGE

Mr. Davis on Cruelty to Prisoners.—Mexico.—Turtle on the Southern Coast.—The Southern Leaders an Aristocracy.—Lecture on the Fine Arts, by a Strange Man in a Strange Place 96

CHAPTER IX.

Mr. Davis on Gen. Butler and Dutch Gap.—He denies that Secession was Treason.—His opinion of Grant, McClellan, Pope, and other Union Officers; also of Bragg, Lee and Pemberton.—His Flight from Richmond and Arrest 109

CHAPTER X.

Diseases of the Eye.—Guards removed from the Prisoner's Room.—Mr. Davis takes his first Walk on the Ramparts.—The Policy of Conciliation. —Mr. Davis on Improvements in Land and Naval Warfare 132

CHAPTER XI.

Mr. Lincoln's Assassination.—Ex-President Pierce.— Torture of being Constantly Watched.—Mr. Davis on the Members of his Cabinet and the Opponents of his Administration.—Touching Tribute to the Memory of "Stonewall" Jackson . . . 147

CHAPTER XII.

Mr. Davis seriously Ill.—Restrictions on Correspondence with his Wife.—Clement C. Clay.—A Rampart Interview.—Religious Phase of Mr. Davis' Character 164

Contents

CHAPTER XIII.

PAGE

Southern Migration to Mexico.—Mr. Calhoun's Memory
vindicated from one Charge.—Tribute to Albert
Sidney Johnston.—Failure of Southern Iron-clads
and Loss of the Mississippi 178

CHAPTER XIV.

Mr. Davis on Negro Character.—The Assassination of
President Lincoln.—How the Prisoner's Food was
Served.—A Solemn and Interesting Statement . 191

CHAPTER XV.

Southern Non-Belligerents.—The Ant-Lion and its
Habits.—Mr. Davis on the Future of the Southern
Blacks 203

CHAPTER XVI.

Mr. Davis on Fenianism.—Highly Important.—His
Views of Reconstruction 215

CHAPTER XVII.

Mr. Davis seriously Ill.—Change of Quarters officially
Recommended.—The Pictures and Poetry of the
Bible.—Lafayette's Imprisonment.—Marvellous
Memory and great Variety of Knowledge.—Mr.
Davis on Female Lecturers.—The True Mission of
Women 224

CHAPTER XVIII.

Mr. Davis on Sensation News.—The Condition of the
Negro.—Gen. Butler at Drury's Bluff.—Bishop
Lynch and the Sisters of Charity.—A Story after
the manner of President Lincoln . . . 242

11

Contents

CHAPTER XIX.

Treason.—State and National.—The Fish-Hawk and Bald-Eagle.—Mr. Davis on Senator Benton, Ex-President Buchanan, and President Andrew Johnson.—Preparations to remove Mr. Davis to Carroll Hall 255

CHAPTER XX.

Visit to Richmond.—General Lee.—Mr. Davis on Horseback Exercise.—Macaulay's Pictorial Power . 269

CHAPTER XXI.

Removal to Carroll Hall.—Some Curious Coincidences.—A Foolish Precaution.—Interesting Letter from Mrs. Davis.—Adventures of the Family from Incarceration of Mr. Davis up to Date . . . 281

CHAPTER XXII.

A New Regiment on Guard.—Ordered not to Communicate with Mr. Davis, save on "Strictly Professional Matters."—The Correspondence about Prisoner's Overcoat 301

CHAPTER XXIII.

General Summary in Conclusion.—The Character of Mr. Davis.—Let us be merciful! 314

THE
PRISON LIFE OF JEFFERSON DAVIS

CHAPTER I.

*An Introduction by Anecdote.—The Old-fashioned
Preface in a New Dress.*

LATE one summer evening, hot, hungry, dusty,
thirsty, tired, exasperated, and full of vengeful
thoughts, I was riding down the road from the
bloody and resultless encounter near Bermuda
Hundreds, to where my field hospitals had been
established. Saul journeying to Damascus, breathing out threatenings against his enemies, was in no
fiercer spirit. The day had been oppressively
warm, our losses enormous, our gains nothing;
and worn out with the labor and wretchedness of
superintending the removal of the wounded, I
was cantering wearily but rapidly back to where
many hundred sufferers, in all stages of mangle-
ment, lay awaiting the painful remedy of the
surgeon's art.. Never before had the rebellion,

with its attendant horrors, appeared so inhuman to my mind; and if the hot hatreds of my soul could have taken shape in words, I would have exclaimed, addressing the Confederates under Beauregard:

> " Oh, that each slave had forty thousand lives,
> One is too poor, too weak for my revenge ! "

Half way between the battle-field and my hospitals, I overtook four of our boys in blue, under a corporal, tenderly carrying to the rear a stretcher on which lay a wounded rebel.

Something tempted me to halt and dismount. God forgive me if it was a desire to assure myself that all the suffering had not been on our side. If so, the unworthy feeling was of brief duration; for no sooner, throwing the reins to my orderly, did I stand beside the litter and gaze upon the pale pinched features of the wounded man, than all promptings of patriotic hatred vanished; and there was nothing left in my existence but the deep, overwhelming sympathy of the medical man for a patient needing aid to call him back from death.

He needed aid, indeed. His left arm was shot through; his right leg shattered and badly mangled above the ankle; his hip was torn by the fall of his horse, and life appeared fast ebbing. In his horse, by the way, as it fell under him, there were sixteen bullets. He had ridden right in on top of the 6th Conn. regiment, and our boys had given him what we called "a blizzard." *

"My poor man," I said, "you are wounded nearly unto death."

"I feel it," he faintly replied. "I am General Walker, of Beauregard's staff. Let me rest somewhere, and dictate some last words to my Wife and Commander."

Where was my hatred now? Where the fierce thirst of retribution that should have looked on this unfortunate's agony as a just judgment?

Giving him some brandy from a pocket-flask, I told the corporal in charge to carry him to my own tent, next General Gillmore's head-quarters at Hatcher's House; and hastily scribbling a line to my hospital steward, "Take charge—will be with you soon," I remounted, and galloped off to the sickening scenes always presented in a field hospital after a severe engagement.

It was midnight, or some little later, before my

---

* Since the publication of this book attention has been called to the fact that the word "blizzard" was here for the first time used to describe a storm of any kind.

duties to the hundreds of our boys would allow me to visit the sufferer in my tent. His case needed immediate amputation of the lower leg, and there was no sufficient light for performing the operation.

"Tear down that smoke-house and kindle a big bonfire," was my order. "We must get light somehow, and quickly, or this man will die. He is seven-eighths on his way to death already."

Never before had I been so painfully anxious. The feeling arose, no doubt, from an instinct of conscience punishing my unprofessional thoughts —or half thoughts—when first halting beside his litter. The man had to be saved, or an unhappy recollection would haunt my life. No appliance that care or skill could furnish must be wanting. It had been against Beauregard all day that my anger had been specially kindled. I recalled our first defeat at Bull Run. His memorable "beauty and booty" proclamation. Was I always to witness defeat when opposed to this enemy? And it was against Beauregard and all belonging to him, that day, while the contest lasted, that the imprecations of my soul, if not uttered, had been most vehemently felt.

But here now was a military part of Beauregard —one of his eyes or arms—over whom I yearned as if with a brother's sympathy. My business was to heal the wounded, not to wound. By what right had I indulged the vengeful thoughts which filled my breast when first meeting on the road this shattered human wreck?

The bonfire was soon blazing, and before the operation commenced—as a happy result could scarce be hoped—I procured an amanuensis for General Walker, to whom he hurriedly dictated two letters. They were farewells to his Wife and General Beauregard. Will the loyal world think worse of me, if I confess, that while hearing the few feeble whispers in which this wounded rebel communicated to a strange soldier of the hostile force what he expected to be his last words on earth —his last messages to the Commander he reverenced, and the Wife he was to see no more— I found an unusual moisture making my sight uncertain?

General Walker, however, was not destined to die. By the flickering light of the bonfire, and with the aid of Surgeons Janeway and Buzelle, the amputation was successfully performed, and

17

his other wounds properly treated. He remained at once my guest and patient until sufficiently restored for safe transfer to the General Hospital at Fortress Monroe, and is now hopping around the earth somewhere, blithe and hearty on the leg that is left him; perfectly willing to be "reconstructed," I should imagine, in more senses than one; nor any the less likely in future to make a loyal citizen, from such recollections as he may yet preserve of the bonfire and the tent, the amanuensis and the attending doctors of that midnight scene.

This is the material part of my preface, and contains the only apology I shall offer in case any over-sensitively loyal readers may feel, or affect to feel, shocked on finding in the following pages some record of the imprisonment of Jefferson Davis, not written to gloat over the misfortunes of a fallen enemy—certainly not aiming to palliate his political or other errors; but to depict so much of him as was revealed to the Writer during a medical attendance of many months while Mr. Davis lay a prisoner in Fortress Monroe. Should any such objectors be found, the Writer believes himself safe in predicting that they will be drawn pretty exclusively from that loyal class who were non-belligerent, except in the contracting line, and strictly non-combatant, save for higher percentages of profit, during the recent contest for the Union.

———

For the rest, the following pages have been prepared from a conscientious conviction of duty, under the advice of eminent and respected friends, and with the sanction of many gentlemen in our public life, who are not more exalted by station than by loyalty, intelligence, and moral worth.

The book aims to introduce no discussion of any political questions connected with the late rebellion; nor to be a plea influencing public judgment, either for or against, the gentleman who was for so many months the Author's patient. It will report him as he was seen during a protracted and confidential medical attendance, extenuating nothing of public interest, and setting down naught in malice.

Of course, the relations of physician and patient have a sacredness of confidence which the Writer would be the last to violate; and all such restrictions, in this volume, will be found rigidly observed. No knowledge gained during such relationship that might injure Mr. Davis if published, could properly or without flagrant infidelity, be given to the world by his medical attendant; and it is from a sincere conviction that the reverse must prove the fact, and from a sincere personal sympathy and respect for the subject of this memoir, that the present volume has been undertaken.

It may here be proper to remark—less partisan malice should attempt from interested motives to distort the Writer's position—that he has been through all the years of his thinking life an earnest and active opponent of slavery, and of all the other cardinal doctrines on which the leaders of the late Rebellion claimed to base their action. He was a member of the Republican party from its birth down to the present day—an uncompromising supporter of the Union; and it is from his deep conviction that the Union can best be reconstructed, and its harmony of relationship restored, by pursuing a moderate policy and seeking to understand, in their present frame of mind, what are the views of the men who were recently our leading enemies, that he would now beg the earnest attention of all classes in the Country to such portions of this volume as shadow forth the opinions of Mr. Davis in regard to the future of the South.

CHAPTER II.

Fortress Monroe.—The Ceremonial of delivering Mr. Davis into Custody.—His first Day in the Casemate.

FORTRESS MONROE is too well known to need any description in these pages. It is the most powerful regular fortification on the Continent; and, with its subordinate works is the grim Cerberus guarding the approach by water to our National Capital. It has witnessed the initial movements of many most interesting chapters in the recent war, though itself never within reach of hostile guns, save when the *Merrimac* made its brief raid upon our fleet in Hampton Roads—the raid so notably checked by Captain Worden in his little Monitor.

Either from it, or past it from Annapolis, had sailed the chief expeditions, marine and military, of the Southern coast. Beneath its ramparts the transports of McClellan's army had made brief rendezvous when hastening to the campaign of the Peninsula; and here again they had to pass,

22

when returning with diminished ranks and soiled plumage, to save the National Capital after General Pope's disaster. It witnessed the sailing of Sherman's Port Royal expedition, to which the writer had the honor to belong; the expeditions of Burnside, Butler, Banks, and all the other joint military and naval movements which thundered for three years along the coast, from Cape Hatteras to Sabine Pass. Farragut, Du Pont and Porter stepped ashore on its hospitable beach when returning from their most famous exploits.

Of a truth, Fortress Monroe, though not properly in the war, was of the war—a rendezvous for our greatest naval, military and civil chiefs in some of their greatest moments; nor will its least intering reminiscence to the future tourist be this which records, that in one of its granite casemates, and looking out through the bars of a grated embrasure on the Empire he had lost, lay for many months in solitary confinement, and awaiting trial, the defeated Chief of the mightiest rebellion which this earth has yet witnessed; or, at least, the vastest in extent and the most formidable in its resources, of which history gives any clear and credible record.

And never before, indeed, did the old fort witness such excitement, though partially suppressed and held in check by military discipline and the respect due to a fallen enemy, as on the 19th day of May, 1865, when the propeller *William P. Clyde* dropped anchor in Hampton Roads, and the news spread on shore—first in eager, questioning whispers, then in the full assurance of conviction—that she had on board as prisoners Jefferson Davis, late President of the late Confederacy and his family; Alexander H. Stephens, Vice-President; John H. Reagan, late Postmaster-General; Clement C. Clay, and several more State prisoners belonging to his now scattered and ruined house.

"What will they do with him?" "When will they bring him ashore?" "Guess they'll take him right on to Washington and hang him by Military Commission?" "Guess you're a jackass; they can't hang him, unless they hang all." "Jackass yourself; the papers say he was partner with the assassins in killing Lincoln." "Who are the other chaps with him?" "Will they keep him in the woman's toggery he had on when caught?" "Guess there's no truth in that."

"It's just as true as preaching—all the papers say so." "They'll hang Clem. Clay sure." This was something of the conversational buzz I had to pass through, while hastening down from my quarters inside the fort, to get an early view of the little steamer, which, with her imprisoned freight, was the centre of attention.

For the next three days these speculations continued, colloquially and in the papers; but meantime, and for some days previously, preparations had been going on within the fort, under the direction of Colonel Brewerton of the Engineers, which gave evidence to the initiated that the State prisoners on board the propeller in the offing would soon be transferred—at least some of them, and for the present—to securer quarters. Blacksmiths and carpenters were busily at work fitting up casemates number two and four in first front, and near the postern, for the reception of prisoners. They were being partitioned off into regular cells by busy bricklayers; heavy iron bars were placed across the external embrasures, and windows opening on the interior; and the cells intended for the prisoners were partitioned off into two apartments, that next the embrasure being intended for the captives, while the room or cell opening on the interior of the fort was for his guard.

"And it has come to this," was my reflection, as I stood with folded hands first contemplating these arrangements. "But a few months ago, the man for whose reception these preparations are being made, was the acknowledged ruler of many millions of American citizens. He had armies at his command; cabinet officers; a staff of devoted adherents; and ambassadors, though not officially recognised, at all the courts of Europe. Nearly a million of lives—by battle, disease, and starvation—have been sacrificed for, and against, the cause of which he was the chosen representative. And it has come to this with him!" Aye, and was soon to come to worse. But this is anticipating.

On the morning of the 21st of May some of the minor State prisoners on board the *Clyde*—the rebel General Wheeler and his staff—were placed on board the gunboat *Maumee*, which then steamed for Fort Warren in Boston harbor; while Alexander H. Stephens, ex-Postmaster Reagan, and some others were soon after transferred on board the gunboat *Tuscarora*, which immediately started off to Fort Delaware, as was presumed. Intense excitement, on shore and in the neighboring vessels, accompanied all these changes; but Major-General Halleck, who had come down some days before to superintend the arrangements, would make no sign, and speculation consequently ran higher and higher every moment as to whether the chief prisoner of all was destined to remain at the fort, or be transferred elsewhere in custody without halting.

At last, on the afternoon of the 22d, all doubts were set at rest by the arrival of Major-General Miles in a special steamer from Baltimore, this officer being now assigned to the command of the fort, relieving Colonel Roberts; and simultaneously therewith, from the posting of chains of sentinels and guards to keep back the crowd along the Engineer's Landing, and from thence along the route to the Water Battery Postern, it became clear that the important prisoner was about being landed, and that his route would lie in this direction.

The parting between Mr. Davis, his wife, four children, and the other members of his family and household who were on board the *Clyde*, was extremely affecting, as I have been told by officers who were present—the ladies sobbing passionately as the chief prisoners—Messrs. Clay and Davis—were handed over the ship's side and into the boat, which was to convey them, under guard, to their unknown fate.

The procession into the fort was simple though momentous, and was under the immediate inspection of Major-General Halleck and the Hon. Charles A. Dana, then Assistant Secretary of War; Colonel Prichard, of the Michigan cavalry, who immediately effected the capture, being the officer in command of the guard from the vessel to the fort. First came Major-General Miles holding the arm of Mr. Davis, who was dressed in a suit of plain Confederate grey, with a grey slouched hat—always thin, and now looking much wasted and very haggard. Immediately after these came Colonel Prichard accompanying Mr. Clay, with a guard of soldiers in their rear. Thus they passed through files of men in blue from the Engineer's Landing to the Water Battery Postern; and on arriving at the casemate which had been fitted up into cells for their incarceration, Mr. Davis was shown into casemate No. 2 and Clay into No. 4, guards of soldiers being stationed in the cells numbered 1, 3, and 5, upon each side of them. They entered; the heavy doors clanged behind them, and in that clang was rung the final knell of the terrible, but now extinct, rebellion. Here, indeed, is a fall, my countrymen. Another and most striking illustration of the mutability of human greatness. Let me here give a picture of the earliest scene in the cell of Mr. Davis, as related immediately after its occurrence by one who was a passive actor therein, my own connection with Mr. Davis not commencing until two days after (May the 24th), when I was first detailed by Major-General Miles as his attending physician.

Being ushered into his inner cell by General Miles, and the two doors leading thereinto from the guard-room being fastened, Mr. Davis, after surveying the premises for some moments, and looking out through the embrasure with such thoughts passing over his lined and expressive face as may be imagined, suddenly seated himself in a chair, placing both hands on his knees, and asked one of the soldiers pacing up and down within his cell this significant question: "Which way does the embrasure face?"

The soldier was silent.

Mr. Davis, raising his voice a little, repeated the inquiry.

But again dead silence, or only the measured footfalls of the two pacing sentries within, and the fainter echoes of the four without.

Addressing the other soldier, as if the first had been deaf and had not heard him, the prisoner again repeated his inquiry.

But the second soldier remained silent as the first, a slight twitching of his eyes only intimating that he had heard the question, but was forbidden to speak.

"Well," said Mr. Davis, throwing his hands up and breaking into a bitter laugh, "I wish my men could have been taught your discipline!" and then, rising from his chair, he commenced pacing back and forth before the embrasure, now looking at the silent sentry across the moat, and anon at the two silently pacing soldiers who were his companions in the casemate.

What caused his bitter laugh—for even in his best days his temper was of the saturnine and atrabilious type, seldom capable of being moved beyond a smile? Was he thinking of those days

under President Pierce, in which on his approach
the cannon of the fortress thundered their hoarse
salute to the all-powerful Secretary of War, the
fort's gates leaping open, its soldiers presenting
arms, and the whole place under his command?
Or those later days under Mr. Buchanan when,
as the most powerful member of the Military Committee of the Senate, similar honors were paid on
his arrival at every national work—even during
those final moments when he was plotting "to
secure peace" by placing in command of all our
forts and armories such officers as he thought
might be relied upon to "go with the South if
the worst came?"

And was not his question significant:—"which
way does this embrasure face?" Was it north,
south, east, or west? In the hurry and agitation
of being conducted in, he had lost his reckoning
of the compass, though well acquainted with the
localities; and his first question was in effect:
"Does my vision in its reach go southward to the
empire I have lost, or north to the loyal enemies
who have subdued my people?"—for it is always
as "his people" that Mr. Davis refers to the
Southern States.

His sole reading-matter a Bible and prayerbook, his only companions those two silent guards, and his only food the ordinary rations of bread and beef served out to the soldiers of the garrison—thus passed the first day and night of the ex-President's confinement.

CHAPTER III.

Placing Mr. Davis in Irons.—His Protest and his Struggles.—My First Visit to the Prisoner.

On the morning of the 23d of May, a yet bitterer trial was in store for the proud spirit—a trial severer, probably, than has ever in modern times been inflicted upon any one who had enjoyed such eminence. This morning Jefferson Davis was shackled.

It was while all the swarming camps of the armies of the Potomac, the Tennessee, and Georgia —over two hundred thousand bronzed and laurelled veterans—were preparing for the Grand Review of the next morning, in which, passing in endless succession before the mansion of the President, the conquering military power of the nation was to lay down its arms at the feet of the Civil Authority, that the following scene was enacted at Fort Monroe:

Captain Jerome E. Titlow, of the 3d Pennsylvania Artillery, entered the prisoner's cell, followed by the blacksmith of the fort and his assistant, the latter carrying in his hands some heavy and harshly-rattling shackles. As they entered, Mr. Davis was reclining on his bed, feverish and weary after a sleepless night, the food placed near to him the preceding day still lying untouched on its tin plate near his bedside.

"Well?" said Mr. Davis as they entered, slightly raising his head.

"I have an unpleasant duty to perform, Sir," said Captain Titlow; and as he spoke, the senior blacksmith took the shackles from his assistant.

Davis leaped instantly from his recumbent attitude, a flush passing over his face for a moment, and then his countenance growing livid and rigid as death.

He gasped for breath, clutching his throat with the thin fingers of his right hand, and then recovering himself slowly, while his wasted figure towered up to its full height—now appearing to swell with indignation and then to shrink with terror, as he glanced from the captain's face to the shackles—he said slowly and with a laboring chest:

"My God! You cannot have been sent to iron me?"

"Such are my orders, Sir," replied the officer, beckoning the blacksmith to approach, who stepped forward, unlocking the padlock and preparing the fetters to do their office. These fetters were of heavy iron, probably five-eighths of an inch in thickness, and connected together by a chain of like weight. I believe they are now in the possession of Major-General Miles, and will form an interesting relic.

"This is too monstrous," groaned the prisoner, glaring hurriedly round the room, as if for some weapon, or means of self-destruction. "I demand, Captain, that you let me see the commanding officer. Can he pretend that such shackles are required to secure the safe custody of a weak old man, so guarded and in such a fort as this?"

"It could serve no purpose," replied Captain Titlow; "his orders are from Washington, as mine are from him."

"But he can telegraph," interposed Mr. Davis, eagerly; "there must be some mistake. No such outrage as you threaten me with, is on record in the history of nations. Beg him to telegraph, and delay until he answers."

"My orders are peremptory," said the officer,

"and admit of no delay. For your own sake, let me advise you to submit with patience. As a soldier, Mr. Davis, you know I must execute orders."

"These are not orders for a soldier," shouted the prisoner, losing all control of himself. "They are orders for a jailer—for a hangman, which no soldier wearing a sword should accept! I tell you the world will ring with this disgrace. The war is over; the South is conquered; I have no longer any country but America, and it is for the honor of America, as for my own honor and life, that I plead against this degradation. Kill me! kill me!" he cried, passionately, throwing his arms wide open and exposing his breast, "rather than inflict on me, and on my People through me, this insult worse than death."

"Do your duty, blacksmith," said the officer, walking towards the embrasure as if not caring to witness the performance. "It only gives increased pain on all sides to protract this interview."

At these words the blacksmith advanced with the shackles, and seeing that the prisoner had one foot upon the chair near his bedside, his right hand resting on the back of it, the brawny mechanic made an attempt to slip one of the shackles over the ankle so raised; but, as if with the vehemence and strength which frenzy can impart, even to the weakest invalid, Mr. Davis suddenly seized his assailant and hurled him half-way across the room.

On this Captain Titlow turned, and seeing that Davis had backed against the wall for further resistence, began to remonstrate, pointing out in brief, clear language, that this course was madness, and that orders must be enforced at any cost. "Why compel me," he said, "to add the further indignity of personal violence to the necessity of your being ironed?"

"I am a prisoner of war," fiercely retorted Davis; "I have been a soldier in the armies of America, and know how to die. Only kill me, and my last breath shall be a blessing on your head. But while I have life and strength to resist, for myself and for my people, this thing shall not be done."

Hereupon Captain Titlow called in a sergeant and file of soldiers from the next room, and the sergeant advanced to seize the prisoner. Immediately Mr. Davis flew on him, seized his musket and attempted to wrench if from his grasp.

Of course such a scene could have but one issue. There was a short, passionate scuffle. In a moment Davis was flung upon his bed, and before his four powerful assailants removed their hands from him, the blacksmith and his assistant had done their work—one securing the rivet on the right ankle, while the other turned the key in the padlock on the left.

This done, Mr. Davis lay for a moment as if in stupor. Then slowly raising himself and turning round, he dropped his shackled feet to the floor. The harsh clank of the striking chain seems first to have recalled him to its situation, and dropping his face into his hands, he burst into a passionate flood of sobbing, rocking to and fro, and muttering at brief intervals: "Oh, the shame, the shame!"

It may here be stated, though out of its due order—that we may get rid in haste of an unpleasant subject—that Mr. Davis some two months later, when frequent visits had made him more free of converse, gave me a curious explanation of the last feature in this incident.

He had been speaking of suicide, and denouncing it as the worst form of cowardice and folly. "Life is not like a commission that we can resign when disgusted with the service. Taking it by your own hand is a confession of judgment to all that your worst enemies can allege. It has often flashed across me as a tempting remedy for neuralgic torture; but thank God! I never sought my own death but once, and then when completely frenzied and not master of my actions. When they came to iron me that day, as a last resource of desperation, I seized a soldier's musket and attempted to wrench it from his grasp, hoping that in the scuffle and surprise, some one of his comrades would shoot or bayonet me."

What has preceded this, with the exception of the preceding paragraph and of things I saw—such as the cell, procession, etc.—has been based on the evidence of others who came fresh from the scenes they pictured. I now reach the commencement of my personal relations with the prisoner, and for all that follows am willing to be held responsible.

On the morning of May 24th, I was sent for about half-past 8 A.M., by Major-General Miles; was told that State-prisoner Davis complained of being ill, and that I had been assigned as his medical attendant.

Calling upon the prisoner—the first time I had ever seen him closely—he presented a very miserable and afflicting aspect. Stretched upon his pallet and very much emaciated, Mr. Davis appeared a mere fascine of raw and tremulous nerves —his eyes restless and fevered, his head continually shifting from side to side for a cool spot on the pillow, and his case clearly one in which intense cerebral excitement was the first thing needing attention. He was extremely despondent, his pulse full and at ninety, tongue thickly coated, extremities cold, and his head troubled with a long-established neuralgic disorder. Complained of his thin camp mattress and pillow stuffed with hair, adding, that he was so emaciated that his skin chafed easily against the slats; and, as these complaints were well founded, I ordered an additional hospital mattress and softer pillow, for which he thanked me courteously.

"But I fear," he said, as, having prescribed, I was about taking my leave, accompanied by Captain Evans, 3d Pennsylvania Artillery, who was officer of the day; "I fear, Doctor, you will have a troublesome and unsatisfactory patient. One whose case can reflect on you little credit. There are circumstances at work outside your art to counteract your art; and I suppose there must be a conflict between your feelings as a soldier of the Union and your duties as a healer of the sick."

This last was said with a faint smile, and I tried to cheer him, assuring him, if he would only keep quiet and endeavor to get some rest and sleep, which my prescription was mainly addressed to obtain, that he would be well in a few days. For the rest, of course a physician could have no feelings nor recognise any duties but towards his patient.

Mr. Davis turned to the officer of the day, and demanded whether he had been shackled by special order of the Secretary of War, or whether General Miles had considered this violent course essential to his safe-keeping? The Captain replied that he knew nothing of the matter; and so our first interview ended.

On quitting Mr. Davis, at once wrote to Major Church, Assistant Adjutant-General, advising that the prisoner be allowed tobacco—to the want of which, after a lifetime of use, he had referred as one of the probable partial causes of his illness—though not complainingly, nor with any request that it be given. This recommendation was approved in the course of the day; and on calling in the evening brought tobacco with me, and Mr. Davis filled his pipe, which was the sole article he had carried with him from the *Clyde*, except the clothes he then wore.

"This is a noble medicine," he said, with something as near a smile as was possible for his haggard and shrunken features. "I hardly expected it; did not ask for it, though the deprivation has been severe. During my confinement here I shall ask for nothing."

He was now much calmer, feverish symptoms steadily decreasing, pulse already down to seventy-five, his brain less excitable, and his mind becoming more resigned to his condition. Complained that the foot-falls of the two sentries within his chamber made it difficult for him to collect his thoughts; but added cheerfully that, with this—touching his pipe—he hoped to become tranquil.

This pipe, by the way, was a large and handsome one, made of meerschaum, with an amber mouth-piece, showing by its color that it had seen "active service" for some time—as indeed was the case, having been his companion during the stormiest years of his late titular Presidency. It is now in the Writer's possession, having been given to him by Mr. Davis, and its acceptance insisted upon as the only thing he had left to offer.

CHAPTER IV.

*Conversation with Mr. Davis on many Points.—
The Removal of his Shackles demanded as a
Medical Necessity.*

MORNING of 25th May. My patient much easier
and better. Had slept a little, and thanked me
for the additional mattress.

"I have a poor, frail body," he said; "and
though in my youth and manhood, while soldier-
ing, I have done some rough camping and campaigning, there was flesh then to cover my nerves
and bones; and that makes an important difference."

He then spoke of his predisposition to bilious
fever at this period of the year, stating that it
usually began with a slight chill, then ran into a
remittent condition. Had also suffered much
from neuralgia, by which the sight of one eye had
been destroyed; and had been a victim to what
he called "the American malady," dyspepsia, ever
since quitting the active, open-air life of the army.

44

Having ordered him a preparation of Calisaya bark after each meal to assist digestion Mr. Davis spoke familiarly of all the various preparations of this medicine; then digressed into some reminiscence of a conversation he once had with an eminent English physician in regard to antiperiodics.

He took the ground, said Mr. Davis, that Peruvian bark in its various forms was the only reliable therapeutic agent of this kind—and it may be so with the practice in England. Here, however (I told him), we have a number perfectly reliable, such as Salicine, from the willow, a preparation of arsenic (in solution), and so forth.

He appeared anxious to know what agents could be used for adulterating quinine and the other preparations of bark, for that they are grossly adulterated he knew. Taking all the risks of running the blockade, these preparations, or preparations purporting to be such, had been sold at Wilmington and Charlestown during the war, at prices in gold for which the genuine articles could scarcely have been procured in London. They were the best his people could get, however, and very thankful they were when they could be had.

Then spoke of the crime of adulterating medicines as heinous in the extreme, and referred to a speech he had made on the subject in the Senate of the United States, asking legislative interference, and that no adulterated drugs should be allowed to pass the Custom-House. His action had been based, partly on his own acquaintance with the facts, but more especially on a report from an eminent chemist in New York city, setting forth the magnitude of the abuse, with tabular statements.

"There was one restriction of the war," he went on to say, "imposed by the overwhelming superiority of your navy, which I do not believe an enlightened and Christian civilization can approve. I refer to that making medicines contrabrand of war. This inflicted much undeserved suffering on women and children and the whole non-combatant class, while comparatively but little affecting the combatants. For our soldiers we had to procure the requisite medicines, at whatever cost or sacrifice; so that the privation fell chiefly upon those who were not engaged in the war, save as helpless spectators. I am far from saying this restriction was not justified by the laws of war, as heretofore acknowledged and practised; but whenever these laws come to be revised in a spirit more harmonizing with the advanced intelligence of our times, some friend of humanity should plead that cargoes duly vouched as only containing medicines should not be liable to stoppage."

Happening to notice that his coffee stood cold and apparently untasted beside his bed in its tin cup, I remarked that here was a contradiction of the assertion implied in the old army question, "Who ever saw cold coffee in a tin cup?" referring to the eagerness with which soldiers of all classes, when campaigning, seek for and use this beverage.

"I cannot drink it," he remarked, "though fond of coffee all my life. It is the poorest article of the sort I have ever tasted; and if your government pays for such stuff as coffee, the purchasing quartermaster must be getting rich. It surprises me, too, for I thought your soldiers must have the best—many of my Generals complaining of the difficulties they encountered in seeking to prevent our people from making volunteer truces with your soldiers whenever the lines ran near each other, for the purpose of exchanging the tobacco we had in abundance against your coffee and sugar."

Replied that the same difficulty had been felt on our side, endangering discipline and calling for severe measures of repression. The temptation to obtain tobacco was uncontrollable. One of our lads would pop his head up from his rifle-pit and cry: "Hey, Johnny, any tobacco over your way?" to which the reply would instantly come, "Yes, Yank, rafts of it. How is it with you on the coffee question?" A satisfactory reply being given, the whisper would run along each line, "Cease firing, truce for coffee and tobacco;" and in another moment scores of the combatants, on either side, would be scrambling over their respective earthworks, and meeting on the debatable land between, for commercial dicker and barter in true Yankee style.

This picture seemed to amuse the patient. His spirits were evidently improving. Told him to spend as little time in bed as he could; that exercise was the best medicine for dyspeptic patients. To this he answered by uncovering the blankets from his feet and showing me his shackled ankles.

"It is impossible for me, Doctor; I cannot even

stand erect. These shackles are very heavy; I know not, with the chain, how many pounds. If I try to move they trip me, and have already abraded broad patches of skin from the parts they touch. Can you devise no means to pad or cushion them, so that when I try to drag them along they may not chafe me so intolerably? My limbs have so little flesh on them, and that so weak, as to be easily lacerated."

At sight of this I turned away, promising to see what could be done, as exercise was the chief medical necessity in his case; and at this moment the first thrill of sympathy for my patient was experienced.

That afternoon, at an interview sought with Major-General Miles, my opinion was given that the physical condition of State-prisoner Davis required the removal of his shackles, until such time as his health should be established on some firmer basis. Exercise he absolutely needed, and also some alleviation of his abnormal nervous excitement. No drugs could aid a digestion naturally weak and so impaired, without exercise; nor could anything in the pharmacopœia quiet nerves so over-wrought and shattered, while the continual irritation of the fetters was counter-poising whatever medicines might be given.

"You believe it, then, a medical necessity?" queried General Miles.

"I do most earnestly."

"Then I will give the matter attention;" and at this point for the present the affair ended.

May 26th.—Called with the Officer of the Day, Captain James B. King, at 1 P.M. Found Mr. Davis in bed, complaining of intense debility, but could not point to any particular complaint. The pain in his head had left him last night, but had been brought back this forenoon and aggravated by the noise of mechanics employed in taking down the wooden doors between his cell and the exterior guard-room, and replacing these with iron gratings, so that he could at all times be seen by the sentries in the outside room, as well as by the two "silent friends," who were the unspeaking companions of his solitude.

Noticed that the prisoner's dinner lay untouched on its tin plate near his bedside, his meals being brought in by a silent soldier, who placed food on its table and then withdrew. Had remarked before that he scarcely touched the food served to him, his appetite being feeble at best, and his digestion out of order.

Quitting him, called on General Miles, and recommended that I be allowed to place the prisoner on a diet corresponding with his condition, which required light and nutritious food. Consent was immediately given, and I had prepared and sent over from my quarters some tea and toast for his evening's meal.

Calling about 7 P.M., found Mr. Davis greatly improved, the tea and toast having given him, he said, new life. Though he had not complained of the fare, he was very thankful for the change. Remarked in reply that I had observed the food given was not fit for an invalid in his condition, and was happy to say permission had been given me to supply from my own table such diet as he might seem to need. On this he repeated that I had an unequal and perplexing task.

"As a soldier you could soon dispose of me," he said; "but as a master of the healing art all your energies will be taxed; and I sometimes hope —sometimes fear—in vain. You have in me a constitution completely shattered, and of course all its maladies aggravated by my present surroundings.''

He then commenced talking—and let me here say that I encouraged him in this, believing conversation and some human sympathy the best medicines that could be given to one in his state—on the subject of the weather.

How has the weather been—rough or fair? In this huge casemate, and unable to crawl to the embrasure, he could not tell whether the weather was rough or smooth, nor how the wind was blowing.

"All my family are at sea, you are aware, on their way to Savannah: and I know the dangers of going down the coast at this season of the year too well to be without intense alarm. My wife and four children, with other relatives, are on board the *Clyde*, and these propellers roll dreadfully and are poor sea-boats in rough weather.''

He then explained with great clearness of detail, and evidently having studied the subject, why the dangers of going down the coast in rough weather were so much greater than coming north.

Going down, ships had to hug the shore—often running dangerously near the treacherous horrors of Cape Hatteras; while in running north they stood out from land to catch the favoring gulf stream, to avoid which they had to run in shore as close as they could when steering south.

He appeared intensely anxious on this subject, recurring to it frequently and speculating on the probable position of the *Clyde* at this time. "Should she be lost," he remarked, "it will be 'all my pretty chickens and their dam at one fell swoop.' It will be the obliteration of my name and house."

"Mrs. Davis, too," he continued, "has much to contend with. Her sister has been very ill, and her two nurses left her while here, and she could procure no others. My only consolation is, that some of my paroled people are on board, and soldiers make excellent nurses. Soldiers are fond of children. Perhaps the roughness of their camp-life makes the contrasted playfulness of infancy so pleasant. Charles of Sweden, Frederick the Great, and Napoleon, were illustrations of this peculiarity. The Duke of Wellington is the only eminent commander of whom no trait of the sort is recorded."

Talking of propellers, and how badly they rolled in a rough sea, I spoke of one called the *Burnside*, formerly stationed at Port Royal, of which the common remark was, that in every three rolls she went clean round.

"Once," I added, "when her Captain was asked what was her draught of water, he replied that he did not know to an inch the height of her smokestack, but it was from the top of that to her keel."

This, and other anecdotes, amused the patient for some quarter of an hour; and whatever could give his mind a moment's repose was in the line of his cure.

As I was leaving, he asked had I been able to do nothing to pad or cushion his shackles? He could take no exercise, or but the feeblest, and with great pain, while they were on.

To this gave an evasive answer, not knowing what might be the action of General Miles, and fearing to excite false hopes. No such half-way measures as padding would suffice to meet the necessities of his case; while their adoption, or suggestion, might defer the broader remedy that was needed. On leaving, he requested me in the

morning to note how the wind blew, and the prospects of the weather, before paying him my visit.
Until he heard of his family's arrival in Savannah
he could know no peace.

CHAPTER V.

Conversations of some Interest.—The Shackles Removed.—Mr. Davis on Various Scientific Subjects.

MAY 27TH.—Called in the morning with the Officer of the Day, Captain Titlow. Found Mr. Davis in bed, very weak and desponding. He had not slept. Had been kept awake by the heavy surging of the wind through the big trees on the other side of the moat. Appeared much relieved when I told him the breeze was nothing like a storm, though it blew north-easterly, which was favorable to the ship containing his family.

He expressed great concern lest his wife should hear through newspapers of the scene in his cell when he was ironed. Would it be published, did I think? And on my remaining silent—for I knew it had been sent to the newspapers on the afternoon of its transpiring—he interlaced his fingers across his eyes, and ejaculated: "Oh, my poor wife, my poor, poor girl! How the heart-rending narrative will afflict her!"

He remained silent for some moments as I sat beside his bed; and then continued, extending his hand that I might feel his pulse:

"I wish she could have been spared this knowledge. There was no necessity for the act. My physical condition rendered it obvious that there could be no idea that fetters were needful to the security of my imprisonment. It was clear, therefore, that the object was to offer an indignity both to myself and the cause I represented—not the less sacred to me because covered with the pall of a military disaster. It was for this reason I resisted as a duty to my faith, to my countrymen, and to myself. It was for this reason I courted death from the muskets of the guard. The Officer of the Day prevented that result, and, indeed,"—bowing to Captain Titlow—"behaved like a man of good feeling. But, my poor wife! I can see the hideous announcement with its flaming capitals, and cannot but anticipate how much her pride and love will both be shocked. For myself I am resigned, and now only say, 'The Lord reprove them!' The physical inconvenience of these things I still feel (clanking his ankles together slightly under the bed-clothes), but their sense of humiliation is gone. Patriots in all ages, to whose memories shrines are now built, have suffered as bad or worse indignities."

He thanked me for the breakfast that had been sent him, expressing the hope that I would not let my wife be put to too much trouble making broth and toast for one so helpless and utterly wretched.

"I wish, Doctor," said he, "I could compensate you by getting well; but my case is most unpromising. Your newspapers," he went on—this with a grim smile—"should pray for the success of your skill. If you fail, where will their extra editions be—their startling head-lines? My death would only give them food for one or two days at most; while my trial—for I suppose I shall be given some kind of trial—would fatten for them a month's crop of lucrative excitement."

Finding the conversation, or rather his monologue, running into a channel more likely to excite than soothe him—the latter being the object for which I was always willing to listen during the fifteen or twenty minutes these interviews usually lasted while he was seriously ill—I now rose to take my leave, gently hinting that he should avoid such thoughts and topics as much as possible.

He took my remark in a wrong sense, as if I had been hurt at his saying anything that might cast a reflection on the justice that would be dealt to him by my government, or upon the style of journalism in Northern newspapers. But I explained that nothing could be farther from my thoughts: that my counsel was purely medical, and to divert him from a theme that must re-arouse the cerebral excitement we were seeking to allay.

"For the rest, Mr. Davis," I went on, "that Doctor should go to College again who is not ready to listen with interest and attention to whatever subject may be uppermost in his patient's mind, unless convinced that the mind's brooding upon it will do harm, not good. We need ventilation in the world of mind not less than in that of physics. Our thoughts need to go abroad in the minds of other men, and take their exercise in the sunlight and free air of language. The doctrine of confession in the Catholic Church is based on the soundest principles of moral and intellectual hygiene. It is throwing open the doors and windows of the soul, changing the atmosphere, and disinfecting every crevice of the mind of the foul vapors engendered by the close dampness and darkness of secresy. The physician who has not learned to act in this faith should re-commence his education."

Called again at 8 P.M. same day. Mr. Davis still very weak, and had been troubled with several faint, not exactly fainting, spells, his pulse indicating extreme debility. He said the nights were very tedious and haggard. During the day he could find employment reading (the Bible or prayer-book being seldom out of his hand while alone), but during the night his anxieties about his family returned; and the foot-falls of the sentries in the room with him—their very breathing or coughing—continually called back his thoughts, when otherwise and for a moment more pleasantly wandering, to his present situation. He had watched the weather all day with intense interest; and had been cheered to observe from the slant of the rain that the wind appeared to continue north-east, so that he hoped his family were by this time in Savannah.

Then went on to say that he feared, after he had been removed from the *Clyde*, his wife must have suffered the annoyance of having her trunks searched—an unnecessary act, it seemed to him, as, of course, if she had anything to conceal, she could have got rid of it on the passage up.

On my remarking, to soothe him, that no such search was probable, he said it could hardly be otherwise, as he had received a suit of heavy clothes from the propeller; and Gen. Miles, when informing him of the fact, had mentioned that there were quite a number of suits there.

"Now I had none with me but such as my wife placed in her own trunks when she left Richmond, so that her trunks have probably been opened; and I suppose," he added with another grim smile, "that the other clothes to which Gen. Miles referred, are now on exhibition or preserved as 'relics.' My only hope is, that in taking my wardrobe they did not also confiscate that of my wife and children; but I realize that we are like him of old who fell amongst a certain class of people and was succored by the good Samaritan."

"And so, Doctor," he went on, "you think all the miserable details of my ironing have been placed before the public? It is not only for the hurt feelings of my wife and children, but for the honor of Americans that I regret it. My efforts to conceal from my wife the knowledge of my sufferings are unavailing; and it were perhaps better that she should know the whole truth, as probably less distressing to her than what may be the impressions of her fears. Should I write such a letter to her, however, she would never get it."

Sunday, May 28th.—At 11 A.M. this morning was sitting on the porch in front of my quarters when Captain Frederick Korte, 3d Pennsylvania Artillery, who was Officer of the Day, passed towards the cell of the prisoner, followed by the blacksmith. This told the story, and sent a pleasant professional thrill of pride through my veins. It was a vindication of my theory, that the healing art is next only in its sacredness and power to that of the healers of the soul—an instance of the doctrinal toga forming a shield for suffering humanity, which none were too exalted or powerful to disregard. I hastily followed the party, but remained in the outer guard-room while the smith removed the shackles. Did not let Mr. Davis see me then, but retired, thinking it better the prisoner should be left alone in the first moments of regaining so much of his personal freedom.

Called again at 2 P.M. with the Officer of the

Day. Immediately on entering, Mr. Davis rose from his seat, both hands extended, and his eyes filled with tears. He was evidently about to say something, but checked himself; or was checked by a rush of emotions, and sat down upon his bed. That I was gratified by the change I will not deny—and let those in the North into whose souls the iron of Andersonville has entered, think twice before they condemn me. The war was over; the prisons on both sides were empty. If by rigor to Davis we could have softened by a degree the sufferings of a single Union prisoner, I, for one, would have said let our retaliation be so terrible as to bring the South to justice. But now, no sufferings of his could recall the souls that had fled, or the bodies that were wasted and fever-stricken. It would not be retaliation to secure justice, but mere ignoble vindictiveness to further torture this unhappy and shattered man. Besides, as his medical adviser, I could know him in no other capacity; and it then remained to be proved—remains yet to be proved—that he was in any manner of volition or wish responsible for the horrors we deplore. Even Napoleon complained that Virion, and his other commissaries of prisoners, stole the food and other stores furnished for their use; and time must develop whether, and how far, Mr. Davis was responsible for the cruel treatment of our boys.

Thus feeling, I congratulated him on the change, observing that my promise of his soon feeling better was being fulfilled; and he must now take all the exercise that was possible for him, for on this his future health would depend. Captain Korte, too, joined in my congratulations very kindly, and spoke with the frank courtesy of a gentleman and soldier.

In speaking of his present state of health, and the treatment he had formerly been under for the same symptoms, Mr. Davis referred very kindly, and in terms of admiration, to his former friend and medical attendant, Dr. Thomas Miller, of Washington. Also to Dr. Stone, of Washington, who had made a specialty of the eye and its diseases. From him he had received clearer ideas of the power of vision, and the adaptation of the eye to various distances and degrees of light, than from any other source. Referring to his own loss of sight in one eye from leucoma, or an ulceration of the cornea, he said he could discern light with it, but could not distinguish objects.

Entering then into conversation upon optics and acoustics, Mr. Davis spoke on both subjects, but more especially the former, with great familiarity. Referring to the undulating waves by which both light and sound are conveyed, he remarked:

"With what admirable perversity nature has avoided all straight lines and angles—the curve, or waving 'line of beauty,' first discovered to men by Hogarth, being the rule with her in every variety of production. In no leaf, flower, tree, rock, animal, bird, fish or shell that nature has produced, can a straight line, angle, or two lines exactly parallel be found."

Speaking of how greatly the powers of the sight may be increased by practice, Mr. Davis upheld the theory that the brain, too, was also enlarged in its capacities, both physically and intellectually, by continual labor. He pointed to the large brains of nearly all who have been eminent in pursuits involving mental labor, contending that as the labor of the tailor develops the muscles of the right thumb and fore-finger, those of the delver the muscles of the leg, and so forth, so the increased exercise of the brain increased its size. There was a fault in his parallel, he knew, or rather what appeared to be a fault—that we can establish no analogy between the mental and physical phases of existence. Still it was certain that labor enlarged all organs involved in it, so far as we had means of judging; and that while we did not know how the brain acted in its reception or emission of ideas—whether purely passively, or with some physical action, however slight— we did know for certain that the brains of all great intellectual workers were much larger, on the average, than those of men pursuing different callings.

Remarked that with these ideas, he must to a great extent be a believer in phrenology; to which he assented, while at the same time protesting against the charlatanisms which had overlapped, for selfish purposes of gain, what of truth there was in the science. Before the matter could be properly tested, the anatomy of the brain should be made a specialty, and studied with all the assistance of innumerable subjects for many years. But the men who now put themselves forward as professors of the science, had probably never seen the inside of any brain— certainly not of half a dozen—in their lives.

Referring to the stories that were probably being circulated about him in the Northern papers, and the falseness of such stories in general, Mr. Davis instanced what he called the foul false-hood that he had preached and effected the repudiation of the Mississippi bonds.

"There is no truth in the report," he said. "The event referred to occurred before I had any connection with politics—my first entrance into which was in 1843; nor was I at any time a disciple of the doctrine of repudiation. Nor did Mississippi ever refuse to acknowledge as a debt more than one class of bonds—those of the Union State Bank only.

"To show how absurd the accusation is," continued Mr. Davis, "although so widely believed that no denial can affect its currency, take the following facts. I left Mississippi when a boy to go to college; thence went to West Point; thence to the army. In 1835 I resigned, settled in a very retired place in the State, and was wholly unknown, except as remembered in the neighborhood where

I had been raised. At the time when the Union Bank bonds of Mississippi were issued, sold and repudiated—as I believe justly, because their issue was in violation of the State Constitution—I endeavored to have them paid by voluntary contributions; and subsequently I sent agents to England to negotiate for this purpose."

Recurring then to the subject of optics and diseases of the eye—which appeared a favorite with him—Mr. Davis descanted on the curious effects of belladonna on the iris and crystalline lens; stating that, though a valuable remedy when only used as such, it tended to coagulate and produce cataract in the latter when used in excess—as witness the number of cases of this kind of injury amongst the ladies of Italy and Spain, where the article was much used as a toilette adjunct. He spoke of the beautiful provisions of nature for the protection of this organ, illustrating by the third transparent eyelid or membrane which all diving birds drop over the eye when darting swiftly through the air or water, thus protecting the delicate organ from being hurt, while allowing a sufficiency of light to guide them. He could not believe that any living things as a class were deprived of the joy of sunlight; and while the microscope had thus far found no organs that we could recognize as of sight in many classes of living things—shell-fish, worms, and so forth—he believed that they must in some manner be impressible with the alternations of light and darkness. It had so long appeared a question with him whether his own eyesight could be saved, that he had given this subject much attention—or rather reflection; and he quoted from Milton with great pathos several passages on the subject:

> Oh dark, dark, dark, amid the blaze of noon ;
> Irrevocable dark ! total eclipse without the hope of day.

And again:

> Nor to these idle orbs doth sight appear
> Of sun, or moon, or stars, throughout the year,
> Or man, or woman.   Yet I argue not
> Against Heaven's hand or will, nor bate a jot
> Of heart or hope ; but still bear up and steer
> Right onward.

CHAPTER VI.

*Operations on the Southern Coast.—Davis Hears
that he is Indicted and to be Tried.—His Joy.
—Views of his own Defence.*

MAY 29TH.—Called with Captain Bispham, 3d
Pennsylvania Artillery, Officer of the Day. Found
Mr. Davis walking up and down the floor, apparently better—but still laboring under some excitement. He said exercise had already done him
good; had slept much better last night; and
rejoiced to see clear and bright weather again,
though little sunshine entered his cell. Thought
though it did not shine on him, it was shining on
his dear wife and children, safely havened from
the dangers of the ocean.

Complained of the dampness of his cell, as one
probable cause of his illness. The sun could never
dart its influence through such masses of masonry.
Surrounded as the fort was with a ditch, in which
the water rose and fell from three to four feet with
the tide, it was impossible to keep such places
free from noxious vapors.

"I am something of an engineer," he said, "and the causes are obvious. Builders fill in the backs of walls with stone-chips and rubble, insufficiently mortared, through which the tidal water ebbs and falls. When it falls it leaves vacuums of damp air, and when it rises again, this mephitic air, with its gases engendered in closeness, dampness and darkness, is forced upward into the casemates, for no masonry is so perfect as to exclude the permeation of gases.

"I am aware," he went on, "that officers and soldiers and their families have been in the habit of occupying these casemates; but when Secretary of War I issued an order forbidding the practice. Huts or tents are much healthier, more especially for children. The casemates of Fort Pulaski were peculiarly unhealthy, that place being erected on what might be called a shaking-scraw, or sponge of miasmatic vegetation, thoroughly permeated by tidal action. Its foundations had to be pile-driven at an enormous expense of money and labor, and only from the necessities of the coast could such a selection of a site have been justified."

Mentioned that I had been at the siege, and gave him some particulars explanatory of the actual situation at the time of the surrender of Col. Olmstead of the 2d Georgia Volunteers, whom he appeared at first inclined to blame as guilty of a premature capitulation. After all, however, he thought the Colonel was excusable, as further holding-out promised no advantages to compensate its loss, the up-river batteries of our forces making it certain that Tatnall's fleet could render no assistance. The surrender of Port Royal he did not think premature, under the circumstances, because if his people had not retreated when they did, our gunboats, running round the creeks in rear of Hilton Head, Port Royal and St. Helena Islands, would have made retreat impossible; while the troops of our Sherman expedition when landed were more than sufficient to overpower the garrisons. The mistake was that powerful works had not been erected in rear of the islands to cover the ferries, and thus secure uninterrupted communication with the mainland. Had this been attended to in the first instance, there would then have been no excuse for the abandonment of the powerful works designed to protect Port Royal—at least none unless preceded by a more protracted resistance.

Recurring to the subject of his family, Mr. Davis asked me had I not been called upon to attend Miss Howell, his wife's sister, who had been very ill at the time of his quitting the *Clyde*. Replied that Col. James, Chief Quartermaster, had called at my quarters, and requested me to visit a sick lady on board that vessel; believed it was the lady he referred to, but could not be sure of the name. Had mentioned the matter to Gen. Miles, asking a pass to visit; but he objected, saying the orders were to allow no communication with the ship.

Mr. Davis exclaimed this was inhuman. The ladies had certainly committed no crime, and there were no longer any prisoners on board the ship when the request was made, he and Mr. Clay having been the last removed. The lady was very seriously ill, and no officer, no gentleman, no man of Christian or even human feeling, would have so acted. Gen. Miles was from Massachusetts, he had heard, and his action both in this and other matters appeared in harmony with his origin. It was much for Massachusetts to boast that one of her sons had been appointed his jailor;

and it was becoming such a jailor to oppress help-less women and children.

June 1st.—Called with Captain Korte, Officer of the Day, about noon. Had been sent for at 8 P.M., but was away fishing. Mr. Davis was suffering from a numbness of the extremities, which he feared was incipient paralysis. Told him it was merely due to an enfeebled circulation, and recommended bathing and friction.

He asked me what luck fishing, and appeared in better spirits than usual. Had just heard, he said, through an irregular channel, that he had been indicted with Mr. Breckinridge in the District of Columbia, and hoped therefore that he was about to have a constitutional trial—not one by military commission, to which he would not have pleaded, regarding it as foregone murder. The news had reached him through the conversa-tion of some soldiers in the guard-room, who sometimes spoke to each other in loud tones what they wished him to overhear. It was probably in no friendly spirit they had given him this news; but to him it was as welcome as air to the drown-ing.

He then referred to the severity of his treatment, supposing himself at present to be merely held for trial, and not already undergoing arbitrary punishment. As this conversation was a very important one, I took full note of it almost immediately on quitting his cell, and it is now given in very nearly, if not precisely, his own words:

"Humanity supposes every man innocent," urged Mr. Davis, "until the reverse shall be proven; and the laws guarantee certain privileges to persons held for trial. To hold me here for trial, under all the rigors of a condemned convict, is not warranted by law—is revolting to the spirit of justice. In the political history of the world, there is no parallel to my treatment. England and the despotic governments of Europe have beheaded men accused of treason; but even after their conviction no such efforts as in my case have been made to degrade them. Apart, however, from my personal treatment, let us see how this matter stands.

"If the real purpose in the matter be to test the question of secession by trying certain persons connected therewith for treason, from what class or classes should the persons so selected be drawn?

"From those who called the State Conventions,

or from those who, in their respective conventions, passed the ordinance of secession? Or, from the authors of the doctrine of State rights? Or, from those citizens who, being absent from their States, were unconnected with the event, but on its occurrence returned to their homes to share the fortunes of their States as a duty of primal allegiance? Or from those officers of the State, who, being absent on public service, were called home by the ordinance, and returning, joined their fellow-citizens in State service, and followed the course due to that relation?

"To the last class I belong, who am the object of greatest rigor. This can only be explained on the supposition that, having been most honored, I, therefore, excite most revengeful feelings—for how else can it be accounted for?

"I did not wish for war, but peace. Therefore sent Commissioners to negotiate before war commenced; and subsequently strove my uttermost to soften the rigors of war; in every pause of conflict seeking, if possible, to treat for peace. Numbers of those already practically pardoned are those who, at the beginning, urged that the black flag should be hoisted, and the struggle made one of desperation.

"Believing the States to be each sovereign, and their union voluntary, I had learned from the Fathers of the Constitution that a State could change its form of government, abolishing all which had previously existed; and my only crime has been obedience to this conscientious conviction. Was not this the universal doctrine of the dominant Democratic party in the North previous to secession? Did not many of the opponents of that party, in the same section, share and avow that faith? They preached, and professed to believe. We believed, and preached, and practised.

"If this theory be now adjudged erroneous, the history of the States, from their colonial organization to the present moment, should be re-written, and the facts suppressed which may mislead others in a like manner to a like conclusion.

"But if—as I suppose—the purpose be to test the question of secession by a judicial decision, why begin by oppressing the chief subject of the experiment? Why, in the name of fairness and a decent respect for the opinions of mankind, deprive him of the means needful to a preparation of his defence; and load him with indignities which must deprive his mind of its due equilibrium? It ill comports with the dignity of a great nation to evince fear of giving to a single captive enemy all the advantages possible for an exposition of his side of the question. A question settled by violence, or in disregard of law, must remain unsettled for ever.

"Believing all good government to rest on truth, it is the resulting belief that injustice to any individual is a public injury, which can only find compensation in the reaction which brings retributive justice upon the oppressors. It has been the continually growing danger of the North, that in attempting to crush the liberties of my people, you would raise a Frankenstein of tyranny that would not down at your bidding. Sydney, and Russel, and Vane, and Peters, suffered; but in their death Liberty received blessings their lives might never have conferred.

"If the doctrine of State Sovereignty be a dangerous heresy, the genius of America would indicate another remedy than the sacrifice of one of its believers. Wickliffe died, but Huss took up his teachings; and when the dust of this martyr was sprinkled on the Rhine, some essence of it was infused in the cup which Luther drank.

"The road to grants of power is known and open; and thus all questions of reserved rights on which men of highest distinction may differ, and have differed, can be settled by fair adjudication; and thus only can they be finally set at rest."

He then apologized for talking politics to one who should not hear such politics as his; but out of the fulness of the heart the mouth speaketh, and in his joy at the unhoped-for news that he had been indicted, and was to have a trial which he supposed must be public, and which publicity would compel to be not wholly one-sided, there was some excuse for his indiscretion.

To change the subject, he returned to fishing, of which we had been speaking. Was a follower and admirer of the sport, but more in theory than practice. His life had been too busy for the past thirty years to allow his indulging even his most cherished inclinations, except at rare intervals. Izaak Walton had been one of his favorite authors;

and one of the counts he had against Benjamin
Franklin, was the latter's fierce attack on the
gentle fisherman. Indeed Franklin had said
many things not of benefit to mankind. His soul
was a true type or incarnation of the New England character—hard, calculating, angular, unable
to conceive any higher object than the accumula-
tion of money. He was the most material of great
intellects. None of the lighter graces or higher
aspirations found favor in his sight; and with
true New England egotism, because he did not
possess certain qualities himself, they were to be
ignored or crushed out of existence everywhere.
The hard, grasping, money-grubbing, pitiless and
domineering spirit of the New England Puritans
found in Franklin a true exponent. Noble qualities he had, however—courage, truth, industry,
economy and honesty. His school of common
sense was the apotheosis of selfish prudence. He
could rarely err, for men err from excess of feeling,
and Franklin had none. The homely wisdom
of his writings, judged from the material standpoint, could never be surpassed; and while he
confessed to disliking him, he was compelled to
admire his "Poor Richard" from its sinewy force.

Mr. Davis then spoke of the restrictions placed upon his reading, which he supposed must soon terminate if he was to be placed on trial. Books would be indispensable to preparing his defence, nor did he see how he could be denied free intercourse with counsel.

Books, if he could get them, would be a great consolation. True, he had the two best—pointing to his Bible and prayer-book; but the mind could not keep continually at the height and strain of earnestness required for their profitable reading. That the papers and other publications of the day should be denied him, he could understand—though even this would not be right when he was preparing for trial. He would then require to know what phase of public opinion he addressed; for in all such trials—and in this age of publicity there must be two tribunals—one inside, but infinitely the vaster one outside the court-room. To old English or other books for his perusal, what objection could be urged? Such indulgences were given to the worst criminals before trials; and even after conviction the prison libraries were open for their use. A mind so active as his had been for forty years, could not suddenly bring its machinery to a pause. It must either have food, or prey upon itself, and this was his case at present. Except for the purpose of petty torture, there could be no color of reason for withholding from him any books or papers dated prior to the war.

June 7th.—I received the following letter from Mrs. Davis, dated Savannah, June 1st, 1865, to Dr. J. J. Craven, Chief Medical Officer, Fort Monroe, Va.

Savannah, Ga., June 1st, 1865.

Dr. J. J. Craven, *Chief Med. Officer, Fort Monroe, Va.:*

Sir,—Through the newspapers I learn that you are the Surgeon of the post, and consequently in attendance upon Mr. Davis. Shocked by the most terrible newspaper extras issued every afternoon, which represent my husband to be in a dying condition, I have taken the liberty, without any previous acquaintance with you, of writing to you. Perhaps you will let me know from your own pen how he is. Would it trouble you too much to tell me how he sleeps—how his eyes look—are they inflamed?—does he eat anything?

—may I ask what is the quality of his food? Do not refuse my request. It seems to me that no possible harm could accrue to your government from my knowing the extent of my sorrow. And if, perchance, actuated by pity, you do not tell me the worst, the newspapers do, and then the uncertainty is such agony! You will perceive, my dear sir, that I plead with you upon the supposition that you sympathize with our sorrows, and in the sufferings of the man have lost sight of the political enemy, who no longer has the power to do aught but bear what is inflicted.

I will not believe that you can refuse my petition. If you are only permitted to say he is well, or he is better, it will be a great comfort to me, who has no other left. If you are kind to him, may God have you in His holy keeping, and preserve all those sources of happiness to you which have, in one day, been snatched away from,

Yours very respectfully,

VARINA DAVIS.

CHAPTER VII.

Mr. Davis on the New England Character.—Future of the South and Southern Blacks.

JUNE 8TH.—Was called to the prisoner, whom I had not seen for a week. Entered with Captain E. A. Evans, Officer of the Day. Found Mr. Davis relapsing and very despondent. Complained again of intolerable pains in his head. Was distracted night and day by the unceasing tread of the two sentinels in his room, and the murmur or gabble of the guards in the outside cell. He said his casemate was well formed for a torture-room of the inquisition. Its arched roof made it a perfect whispering gallery, in which all sounds were jumbled and repeated. The torment of his head was so dreadful, he feared he must lose his mind. Already his memory, vision, and hearing, were impaired. He had but the remains of one eye left, and the glaring, white-washed walls were rapidly destroying this. He pointed to a crevice in the wall where his bed had been, explaining that he had changed to the other side to avoid its mephitic vapors.

Of the trial he had been led to expect, had heard nothing. This looked as if the indictment were to be suppressed, and the action of a Military Commission substituted. If so, they might do with him as they pleased, for he would not plead, but leave his cause to the justice of the future. As to taking his life, that would be the greatest boon they could confer on him, though for the sake of his family he might regret the manner of its taking.

Talked with Mr. Davis for some time, endeavoring to allay his irritation. The trouble of his head did not arise from the causes he supposed, but from a torpid condition of the liver, and would be at once relieved by a bilious cathartic which I prescribed. It was impossible that any malarial poisons at this season of the year could have influence in his casemate. The ventilation was thorough, the place scrupulously clean; and the very whitewash of which he complained as hurting his eyes, was a powerful disinfectant, if such poisons existed. After the action of the medicine he would look on the world with a more hopeful view. In regard to his expected trial, knew nothing, never had known anything, and even knowing would be forbidden to speak.

He said he had not mentioned the matter to question me, but as an ejaculation of impatience, for which his intolerable pain must bear the blame. He was no stranger to pain, nor easily overcome by it. At Buena Vista, though severely wounded, he kept saddle until the close of the day; but the pain of no wound could compare to this aching fury of the brain.

June 9th.—Called, accompanied by Captain Korte, Officer of the Day. Mr. Davis very well— almost entirely relieved. Said he would believe after this that disquietude could be best reached through the stomach. Had slept well, and was greatly refreshed; his head almost free from pain.

Calling me to the embrasure, he pointed out some dark spots on the slope of the moat opposite, and asked me what they were. Told him they were oysters. He had thought so, but was not sure. Had seen them growing in a stranger place —the branches of trees so heavily fruited with them as almost to break. Told him I had seen the same thing, but only along the coasts of South

Carolina, Georgia, and Florida. In the South the oysters cling to high rocks and drooping branches of trees, only requiring to be submerged for a few hours at high tide; while with us, the frosts of winter compel them to keep in deep water.

Mr. Davis spoke of the Coon oysters of the Southern coast—the long, razor-shaped oysters, growing on high ledges, and referred to the negro version of how the coons obtained their flesh. Their story is, that the coon takes in his mouth a blade of bluebent, or meadow grass, and when the oyster opens his shell, drives the stiletto point of the grass into his flesh, killing him instantly, so that he has no power to close his defences. This, though ingenious, is not true. The coon bites off the thin edges of the shell at one point, and then sucks out all the softer parts of the body.

In regard to the propagation of oysters, had some talk, Mr. Davis thinking the spawn drifted in the water unable to control itself and adhered to the first solid substance—rock, bank, or branch —with which it was brought in contact. This, I explained, was not so; the oyster, for the first three or four days of his life, being a tunicated pteropod, able to swim in any direction he may please. At the end of this first period, when he finds a congenial object to fasten upon, he literally settles down in life and commences building himself a house from which there is no annual "May moving"—no process of ejectment short of death.

Talking of the shell-fish and snails of the Southern coast, Mr. Davis referred to the beautiful varieties of helix (*bullima immaculata*, very rare, and *bullima oblongata*) that may be seen feeding on the wild orange-trees of Florida. Also to the sport of harpooning devil-fish by night, first attracting them to the surface by a fire of pine-knots kindled in a cresset over the bow of the boat. The skin of the largest devil-fish ever known, he said, had been preserved in Charleston, its weight when caught being fourteen hundred pounds. Told him I had seen one caught about two years before weighing over six hundred pounds, and the old negroes of the island said it was the heaviest they had seen. He talked of the molluscs and crustacea of the coast, this appearing a favorite subject, and his remarks being much pleasanter, though of less interest, than when given a political complexion. He possesses a large, varied, and practical education; the geology, botany, and all products of his section appearing to have in turn claimed his attention. Not the superficial study of a pedant, but the practical acquaintance of a man who has turned every day's fishing, shooting, riding, or pic-nicking, to scientific account.

June 10th.—Mr. Davis out of sorts, very ill-tempered. Complained that his clean linen, to be sent over twice a week by General Miles, had not been received. General Miles had taken charge of his clothing, and seemed to think a change of linen twice a week enough. It might be so in Massachusetts. But now even this wretched allowance was denied. The general might know nothing of the matter; but if so, some member of his staff was negligent. It was pitiful they could not send his trunks to his cell, but must insist on thus doling out his clothes, as though he were a convict in some penitentiary. If the object were to degrade him, it must fail. None could be degraded by unmerited insult heaped on helplessness but the perpetrators. The day would come that our people would be ashamed of his treatment. For himself, the sufferings he was undergoing would do him good with his people (the South). Even those who had opposed him would be kept silent, if not won over, by public sympathy. Whatever other opinions might be held, it was clear he was selected as chief victim, bearing the burden of Northern hatred which should be more equally distributed.

Speaking of the negroes, Mr. Davis remarked, as regards their future, he saw no reason why they must die out, unless remaining idle. If herded together in idleness and filth, as in the villages established by our military power, the small-pox, licentiousness, and drunkenness would make short work of them. Wherever so herded, they had died off like sheep with the murrain. But remaining on the plantations, as heretofore, and employed for wages, they were a docile and procreative people, altogether differing from the Indians, and not likely to die out like the latter. Their labor was needed; and though they could not multiply so fast in freedom as under their former wholesome restraints, he saw no good argument for their dying out.

In ten years, or perhaps less, the South will have recovered the pecuniary losses of the war. It has had little capital in manufactures. Its capital was in land and negroes. The land remains productive as ever. The negroes remain, but their labor has to be paid for. Before the war, there had been 4,000,000 negroes, average value, $500 each, or total value, two thousand millions of dollars. This was all gone, and the interest upon it, which had been the profits of the negro's labor in excess of his cost for food, clothing, and medicines. Still their labor remains; and with this, and such European labor as will be imported and such Northern labor as must flow South, the profits of the Southern staples will not be long in restoring material prosperity.

The profits of the cotton crop are enormous. Good bottom lands, such as on the Mississippi and Yazoo rivers, yield a bale of 400 lbs. per acre, and some as high as a bale and a quarter; but this is rare. The uplands throughout Georgia, South Carolina, Alabama, etc., yield about from half to three-quarters of a bale; and under the old system of labor, a good negro averaged ten bales a season. The land of the Sea Islands ran about 200 lbs. to the acre; but its fine, long, silky, and durable staple made it from twice to four times the value of other cotton.

In his freedom, if capable of being made to labor at all, the negro will not average more than six bales a year; but as the price of cotton has more than doubled, and is not likely to recede, even this will yield an enormous profit. Six bales, of 400 lbs. each, will be worth $600 at twenty-five cents per pound, while the cost of this species of labor will be about $150 a year per hand and found —a profit of certainly not less than $300 a year on each black laborer employed.

The land will not pass to any great extent from its former proprietors. They will lease it for a few years to men with capital, and then resume working it themselves; or sell portions of it with the same object, not materially decreasing their own possessions. When the country is quiet and the profits of the crop come to be known, there will be a rush southward from the sterile New England regions and from Europe, only equalled by that to California on the discovery of gold. Men will not stay in the mountains of Vermont and New Hampshire cultivating little farms of from fifty to a hundred acres, only yielding them some few hundreds a year profit for incessant toil, when the rich lands of the South, under

skies as warm and blue as those of Italy, and with
an atmosphere as exhilarating as that of France,
are thrown open at from a dollar and a half to
three dollars per acre. The water-power of the
South will be brought into use by this new immigration, and manufactures will spring up in all
directions, giving abundant employment to all
classes. The happy agricultural state of the
South will become a tradition; and with New
England wealth, New England's grasping avarice
and evil passions will be brought along.

The estimate that a million negroes have died
off during the war, he considered excessive. They
had fled or been dragged away from their old
homes in great numbers; but much less than a
million, he thought, would cover their casualties.
As to any general mingling of the races, nature
had erected ample barriers against the crime.
Depraved white men occasionally had children
by black women; but it was comparatively rare
for mulattoes to have large or healthy families;
and quadroons, though extremely amorous, rarely
had children at all. There could be no danger
that Southern white women of the poorer class,
though left greatly in excess of the white male

population by the war, would either cohabit with or marry negroes. Public sentiment on the point is so strong they dare not do it; nor had they any inclination. It would be regarded South as crimes against nature are regarded in all civilized communities.

The blacks were a docile, affectionate, and religious people, like cats in their fondness for home. The name of freedom had charms for them; but until educated to be self-supporting, it would be a curse. If herded together in military villages and fed on rations gratuitously distributed, rum, dirt, and venereal diseases would devour them off the face of the earth in a few years. With peace established, they would return, in ninety-five cases out of the hundred, to their old plantations, and work for their old masters. Freedom was to them an orgie, of which such as had enjoyed it were rapidly sickening. While health lasted, and idleness was saved its penalty by government support, they might get along well enough. But when sick, starving, and ill-treated, their first wish was a longing to be back with their old masters, and redomiciled on their old plantations. Of this, even during the war, and at penalty of returning to slavery, he had seen many instances—enough to convince him that with freedom assured, or rather its evils to them in their unprepared state better understood—the great majority of the blacks would flock back eagerly.

Mr. Davis said he heard my little daughter had undertaken to be his housekeeper, and sent over his meals. He knew the kind hand of woman was always tenderest in the greatest grief. It only needed they should see misery to wish and labor for its relief, unless some great moral turpitude repelled. He begged me to carry the assurance of his gratitude, and hoped—if he might never see her himself—that his children would some day have opportunity to thank the young lady who had been so kind to their father.

CHAPTER VIII.

Mr. Davis on Cruelty to Prisoners.—Mexico.— Turtle on the Southern Coast.—The Southern Leaders an Aristocracy.—Lecture on the Fine Arts, by a Strange Man in a Strange Place.

JUNE 11TH.—Called with Captain R. W. Bickley, 3d Pennsylvania Artillery, Officer of the Day. Mr. Davis still improving, febrile symptoms abated, and had slept, for him, very well the night before. Thanked me for some fruit sent with his breakfast, and then spoke of the fruits of the tropics and their beautiful adaptation to the wants of the inhabitants. Also of Mexico, its climate and productions; a land for which God had done everything, and "where only man was vile." Considered the Mexicans not capable of self-government; they must be cared for, and it belonged to America to protect them. Had the South succeeded without the help of France, this would have been one of his first cares, and he should not have hesitated a moment. The South having

96

failed, leaving the North more powerful than ever, the duty of establishing a continental protectorate was imperative, and could not long be evaded.

Mr. Davis remarked that when his tray of breakfast had been brought in that morning, he overheard some soldiers in the guard-room outside commenting on the food given our prisoners during the late war. To hold him responsible for this was worse than absurd—criminally false. For the last two years of the war, Lee's army had never more than half, and was oftener on quarter rations of rusty bacon and corn. It was yet worse with other Southern armies when operating in a country which had been campaigned over any time. Sherman, with a front of thirty or forty miles, breaking into a new country, found no trouble in procuring food; but had he halted anywhere, even for a single week, must have starved. Marching every day, his men eat out a new section, and left behind them a starving wilderness.

Colonel Northrop, his Commissary-General, had many difficulties to contend with; and, not least, the incessant hostility of certain opponents of his administration, who, by striking at Northrop,

really meant to strike at him. Even General ——,
otherwise so moderate and conservative, was
finally induced to join this injurious clamor.
There was food in the Confederacy, but no means
for its collection, the holders hiding it after the
currency had become depreciated; and, if collected, then came the difficulty of its transportation. Their railroads were overtaxed, and the
rolling-stock soon gave out. They could not feed
their own troops; and prisoners of war in all
countries and ages have had cause of complaint.
Some of his people confined in the West and at
Lookout Point, had been nearly starved at certain
times, though he well knew, or well believed, full
prison-rations had been ordered and paid for in
these cases.

Herd men together in idleness within an inclosure, their arms taken from them, their organization lost, without employment for their time,
and you will find it difficult to keep them in good
health. They were ordered to receive precisely
the same rations given to the troops guarding
them; but dishonest Commissaries and Provost-
Marshals were not confined to any people. Doubtless the prisoners on both sides often suffered that

the officers having charge of them might grow rich; but wherever such dishonesty could be brought home, prompt punishment followed. General Winder and Colonel Northrop did the best they could, he believed; but both were poorly obeyed or seconded by their subordinates. To hold him responsible for such unauthorized privations was both cruel and absurd. He issued order after order on the subject, and, conscious of the extreme difficulty of feeding the prisoners, made the most liberal offers for exchange—almost willing to accept any terms that would release his people from their burden. Non-exchange, however, was the policy adopted by the Federal Government—just as Austria, in her later campaigns against Frederick the Great, refused to exchange; her calculation being, that as her population was five times more numerous than Prussia's, the refusal to exchange would be a wise measure. That it may have been prudent, though inhuman, situated as the South was, he was not prepared to deny; but protested against being held responsible for evils which no power of his could avert, and to escape from which almost any concessions had been offered.

Anxious to hear the opinion of Mr. Davis about the future of Mexico, I brought back the conversation to that point, suggesting that when the country became quiet, and with our continual influx of European immigration, we might have men and enterprise enough to resettle Mexico, and colonize out the present indolent and inefficient race.

"The programme might answer," he thought, "for the thinly peopled parts, though even there its fulfillment must be in the remote future. When the Valley is reached, however, the population is comparatively dense—twenty to the square mile; and political economy teaches that no people so numerous can be crushed out by colonization. A new race must come in to master and guide them, using the present generation as hewers of wood and drawers of water, while educating the next generation for a happier and more intelligent future. It was on a recognition of this necessity the French Emperor based his scheme of European protection; but in failing to make terms with the seceded States, and support them in their struggle, he proved that his comprehension was not equal to the problem. The failure of the

South rendered a future of European rule for Mexico impossible."

June 14th.—Visited prisoner in company with Captain Evans, Officer of the Day. Prescribed for some slight return of nervous headache and sleeplessness. Referring to our previous conversation about the shell-fish, etc., of the Southern coast, Mr. Davis said that books of a scientific nature, if allowed him, would keep his attention occupied, and could do no harm. Would be glad to have a few volumes on the conchology, geology, or botany of the South, and was at a loss to think how such volumes could endanger his safe-keeping.

Said that the loggerhead-turtle appeared a contradiction of the rule that nature makes no vain effort—nothing that had not a perceivable use. Here, however, was an animal averaging from one to three hundred pounds weight, very plentiful from Hatteras to the Gulf, for which human ingenuity had yet found no use. But what part it may perform in the economy of the ocean must of course remain a mystery. That it had some useful mission amongst the denizens of the deep, all analogy would lead us to believe. Early in the spring they come up from the Caribbean Sea and Gulf of Mexico, only approaching the shore to lay their eggs when the high tide serves just after dusk of the evening. The male then remains at the edge of the surf, while the female crawls up the beach to find a proper place for laying. The place being selected, she first makes a hole with her head; then increases its size to about that of a peck measure, by putting one of her forefins into it, and twisting herself around until the required space has been scooped out. The eggs are then laid, about 200 in number, nearly the bulk of a hen's egg each, but with a soft, pliable, and very tough white skin. This done, she packs sand over them to the proper depth, and smoothes the place by crawling over it several times with heavy pressure.

Of these eggs, when undisturbed, about eighty per cent. are hatched; in some four or five weeks swarms of little turtle suddenly breaking out, each about the size and color of a ginger-snap, and hurrying towards the water with infallible instinct. The eggs have three active and powerful enemies—the coon, the crow, and the negro. The coon hunts the turtle-nest by smell, as a certain breed of dogs in France hunt the truffle, and having taken his first meal, leaves the nest open to the crows, who are not long in finishing what may be left. The negroes search the shores every morning at daylight in this season, and when they find the track made by a turtle's flippers follow it up to where the nest is buried, prodding into the sand with a long stick until it is found, and carrying off the contents. The loggerhead is famous for its longevity, and occasionally weighs from four to six hundred pounds.

Speaking of the peculiarities of his people— as he always styled the late Confederate States— Mr. Davis said they were essentially aristocratic, their aristocracy being based on birth and education; while the men of the North were democratic in the mass, making money the basis of their power and standard to which they aspired. It always commanded a premium socially, and was accepted in lack of other qualities. No matter how ill-bred or base, no man possessed of wealth who had not been made judicially infamous, was excluded from northern society. This money-element entered into the politics of the North, while at the South it was, and always had been, powerless. At northern primary elections and nominating conventions, the reins were for him who had money to pay for being allowed control; and the power thus obtained by money was used to get back what it had cost, and to treble that sum during its tenure.

Birth is a guarantee we do not ignore in raising stock, nor should we in growing men. Which should be more important—the pedigree of a horse on which we stake our money, or that of a man we are asked to select for some position of control? The basis of political prominence at the North has been money first, and secondly loquaciousness, effrontery, the arts of the demagogue; while at the South—except in the case of shining talents lifting some individual to eminence by their force —birth, education, and representative rather than noisy or showy qualities, formed the ladder to distinction. No one could fail to be impressed with this difference while attending our National Conventions, Congress, or any other body in which the two sections were represented. He must not be misunderstood as wishing to imply that we had no good blood, no education, no culture at the North—far from it, for he knew we had all in abundance; but under our political system, and owing to the vast influx of a foreign population, they were excluded from our public or representative life. In a word, prominence at the North has, of late, been obtained either by money of the man made prominent, or that he served the money interests of those who pushed his elevation. This evil must continually increase with the increase of immigration; while at the South, birth, education, and intelligence had been the chief usual elements of political distinction— the first necessity being, however, that the man selected should be a true representative of the views of his constituency, whether those views were right or wrong according to northern notions.

To this representative quality, Mr. Davis went on, were due the various positions with which the South had honored him. His selection to the chief office of the Confederacy was in no manner sought. The reasons inspiring the choice were obvious. He was a Mississippian; had graduated at the Military Academy; served with some distinction in the Mexican war; had large experience in the military committee of the Senate, and in the War Department. But one of his chief recommendations lay in this, that after the removal of

Calhoun and General Quitman by death, he became the chief exponent or representative of those principles of State Sovereignty which the South cherished, and of which, as he claimed, the Fathers of the country had been the founders, Thomas Jefferson the inspired prophet, and they the eloquent apostles. He was certainly not more responsible for his own elevation than any of those who had voted to make him President.

June 17th.—Visited Mr. Davis with Captain Korte, Officer of the Day. General Miles, learning that the pacing of the two sentinels in his room at night disturbed Mr. Davis and prevented his sleeping, gave orders that the men should stand at ease during their two hours of guard, both night and day, instead of pacing their accustomed beat. This, Mr. Davis said, was much pleasanter for him, but cruel for the men obliged to stand so long in one position, as if they had been bronze or marble statues. Feared, as it cost them suffering, it would make them hate him more, as the cause—though innocent—of their inconvenient attitude; and there were plenty of men wearing uniforms of that color who hated him more than enough already.

From this point Mr. Davis glided off to some considerations of statuary, commenting on the growing taste for representing animals, birds and men, in painful or impossible attitudes in the *basso-relievos*, bronzes, and other ornaments of modern sculpture. Stricken deer contorted by death-wounds; horses with sides lacerated by the claws of a clinging tiger; partridges, or other birds, choking in snares or pierced with arrows; dying Indians, wounded gladiators, dying soldiers —pain or death in every variety of grade, seemed to form the present staple for popular bronze and Parian ornament. Our sculptors made their horses stand eternally with fore-paws poised in air in an attitude only possible for a moment to the living animal. Such works were not pleasing, but the reverse. They fretted the sensibilities with petty pain, and lacked the repose which should form the chief charm of scuplture. The groups of the Laocoon and Dying Gladiator were the only eminent works of antiquity of which he had heard or seen casts, in which pain or horror had been the elements depicted; and in these the treatment had been so overwhelmingly grand as to numb the sense of suffering by the splendor

of their beauty. For modern sculpture, however
—the statuary designed for parlor ornaments—
he wished to see more pleasant themes. The
agony of a wounded deer or bird could have nothing to recommend it but the fidelity of imitation
with which the agony was portrayed; while in the
Laocoon, there was the titanic struggle of the
father to free his children from the coils of the
serpent, and behind the Dying Gladiator rose up
the gazing circles of the amphitheatre—each
subject wakening trains of thought and emotion
which concealed our sense of physical pain, or only
allowed it to obtrude as a sort of undertone, or
diapason, to the awful beauty of the picture.

Mr. Davis, on this subject, was really eloquent,
showing a keen appreciation of art, and I only
regret that my notes report him so imperfectly.
It struck me as a strange place for such a disserta-
tion, a strange man strangely circumstanced to
be its author, and a strange incident—two armed
soldiers standing like statues within a cell, to
have given origin in such a mind to a lecture on
the æsthetics of repose applied to modern sculpture.

CHAPTER IX.

Mr. Davis on Gen. Butler and Dutch Gap.—He denies that Secession was Treason.—His Opinion of Grant, McClellan, Pope, and other Union Officers; also of Bragg, Lee and Pemberton.— His Flight from Richmond and Arrest.

JUNE 18TH.—Called on Mr. Davis with Captain Jerome E. Titlow, Officer of the Day. Found him continuing to improve in general health—much stronger than he had been on his arrival. Complained of a stricture or tightening of the chest, accompanied by a dry cough. Ordered him to exercise his arms by swinging them back and forth horizontally twice or thrice a day.

Standing at the embrasure, the white sails of a passing vessel suggested the trade and commerce of the James, for the mouth of which it appeared steering. Together in fancy we reascended the banks of the river, with which Mr. Davis was familiar. He asked the fate of all the beautiful plantations along its shores; of Brandon belonging

109

to the Harrisons on the south bank, a place Gen. Butler had harried; of Westover; and beautiful Shirley on the north bank, just opposite Bermuda Hundreds, belonging to that noble Virginian of the old school, Mr. Hill Carter. Told Mr. Davis it was the only one left standing, in all its beautiful antiquity, of the palaces that once lined the James. Carter had been kind to the wounded of McClellan's soldiers and had taken no part in the war, though very possibly a Southern man in sentiment. His place consequently had been not only spared from incursion, but guarded with jealous care by daily details, and was the green spot in the desert made by the movements of contending armies.

Talking of Gen. Butler, said Mr. Davis, with a smile, Richmond owes him something, if only for giving it the best joke of the war. He referred to the Dutch Gap Canal, considered as a war-measure, for as a commercial one, improving the navigation of the James, it was full of advantage. It was a task imposing great hardships upon many thousand soldiers; and must have been inspired by Grant's similar attempt to change the course of the Mississippi at Vicksburg. If successful, the canal only avoided one battery, Fort Howlett, which might have been carried by a resolute effort; nor could any of us understand what adequate object could be gained by it when completed. The James, from Dutch Gap to Richmond, was too shallow for gun-boats; was paved with torpedoes, and obstructed in every conceivable manner. Besides, the works at Chapin's and Drury's Bluffs would still remain.

Commercially, the canal might be of great value to Richmond. The loop of the river which it cut off—about seven miles in length—formed the shallowest and most intricate part of its navigation, from Rockett's to the sea. By making a lock of the Dutch Gap Canal, and throwing a dam across the river just below the higher lock, the water up to Richmond might be permanently raised two feet and placed beyond tidal influence, thus allowing vessels of ten or eleven feet draft to reach the city in all stages of the tide, while at present vessels drawing even eight or nine feet can only with extreme difficulty be brought up at high tide. Commercially, the canal was good; but as a war-measure, of no value.

Mr. Davis said it was contrary to reason, and the law of nations, to treat as a rebellion, or lawless riot, a movement which had been the deliberate action of an entire people through their duly organized State governments. To talk of treason in the case of the South, was to oppose an arbitrary epithet against the authority of all writers on international law. Vattel deduces from his study of all former precedent—and all subsequent international jurists have agreed with him—that when a nation separates into two parts, each claiming independence, and both or either setting up a new government, their quarrel, should it come to trial by arms or by diplomacy, shall be regarded and settled precisely as though it were a difference between two separate nations, which the divided sections, *de facto*, have become. Each must observe the laws of war in the treatment of captives taken in battle, and such negotiations as may from time to time arise shall be conducted as between independent and sovereign powers. Mere riots, or conspiracies for lawless objects, in which only limited fractions of a people are irregularly engaged, may be properly treated as treason, and punished as the public good may require; but Edmund Burke had exhausted argument on the subject, in his memorable phrase, applied to the first American movement for independence: "I know not how an indictment against a whole people shall be framed."

But for Mr. Lincoln's untimely death, Mr. Davis thought, there could have been no question raised upon the subject. That event—more a calamity to the South than North, in the time and manner of its transpiring—had inflamed popular passions to the highest pitch, and made the people of the section which had lost their chief now seek as an equivalent the life of the chief of the section conquered. This was an impulse of passion, not a conclusion which judgment or justice could support. Mr. Lincoln, through his entire administration, had acknowledged the South as a belligerent nationality, exchanging prisoners of war, establishing truces, and sometimes sending, sometimes receiving, propositions for peace. On the last of these occasions, accompanied by the chief member of his cabinet, he had personally met the Commissioners appointed by the Southern States to negotiate, going half way to meet them not far from where Mr. Davis now stood; and the negotiations of Gen. Grant with Gen. Lee, just preceding the latter's surrender, most distinctly and clearly pointed to the promise of a general amnesty; Gen. Grant, in his final letter, expressing the hope that, with Lee's surrender, "all difficulties between the sections might be settled without the loss of another life," or words to that effect.

To my question what he thought of General Grant, Mr. Davis replied that he was a great soldier beyond doubt, but of a new school. If he had not started with an enormous account in bank, his checks would have been dishonored before the culmination was reached. At Shiloh he was defeated the first day; and would have been destroyed or compelled to surrender next morning, but for Buell's timely arrival with a fresh and well-disciplined reinforcement, the strength of which had been variously stated.

When Secretary of War, he thought McClellan the ablest officer in the army, and had employed him on two important services—as Military Commissioner in the Crimea, and to explore a route for the Pacific railroad—both of which duties had been discharged in a manner to increase his reputation. He organized the Army of the Potomac admirably, but it required a com-

mander of more dash to wield the weapon in the
field. McClellan's caution amounted very closely
to timidity—moral timidity, for he was personally
brave. On his first landing in the Peninsula
there had been only 7,000 troops to meet him,
and these he should have rushed upon and overwhelmed at whatever cost. Cautious, and wishing to spare the blood of his men, he commenced
a regular siege at Yorktown giving his enemies
time to concentrate sufficient numbers and drive
him back. As a magnanimous enemy he respected
McClellan, but thought he had been promoted too
rapidly for his own good—before he had ripened
in command and gained the experience requisite
for the supreme position. Had he been kept in a
subordinate capacity the two first years of the
war, rising from a division to a corps, and thence
to command in chief, he would have been the
greatest of our soldiers. He had the best natural
gifts and highest intellectual training, and was
just becoming fitted, and the best fitted, for his
position when removed. Had he been supported
by the government he might have taken Richmond two years earlier, and it was with joy Mr.
Davis heard of his removal after the battles of

South Mountain and Antietam. Such sacrifices of officers to the ignorance of an unwarlike people, anxious to find in him a scapegoat for their own lack of discipline or endurance, were unavoidable in the early stages of every popular war.

Pope, while Secretary of War, he had never been able to make serviceable, and Pope held his own gallantly. His mind was not less inflated than his body. He was a kind of American gascon, but with good scientific attainments. Sumner and Sedgwick were gallant and able soldiers —excellent commanders in action, courteous and reliable in all the relations of life. Hunter, of whom I asked him specially as one of my old commanders, was his beau ideal of the military gentleman—the soul of integrity, intrepidity, true Christian piety and honor. Mr. Davis had long been associated with him, both in the service and socially, and believed Hunter's want of success due in a great measure to his unwillingness to bend to anything mean or sinister. He was rash, impulsive; a man of action rather than thought; yielding to passions which he regarded as divine instincts or intuitions—the natural temper of a devotee or fanatic.

Of the officers on the Confederate side, Mr. Davis spoke in high terms of General Lee, as a great soldier and pure, Christian gentleman; also, in praise of Bragg and Pemberton, though the two latter, from unavoidable circumstances and the hostility of the party opposed to Mr. Davis, had not been accorded the position due to their talents by public opinion in either section. Pemberton made a splendid defence of Vicksburg, and might have been relieved if the officer commanding the army sent to relieve him (General Johnson) had not failed to obey the positive orders to attack General Grant which Mr. Seddon, then Secretary of War, had sent. If the same officer, who was upheld in command by the anti-administration party, had vigorously attacked Sherman at Atlanta when directed, the fortunes of the war would have been changed, and Sherman hurled back to Nashville, over a sterile and wasted country—his retreat little less disastrous than Napoleon's from Moscow. He did not do so, and was relieved—General Hood, a true and spirited soldier, taking his place—but the opportunity was then gone; and to this delay, more than to any other cause, the Southern people will attribute their overthrow, whenever history comes to be truly written.

Bragg's victory over Rosecrans at Chickamauga, Mr. Davis regarded as one of the most brilliant achievements of the war, considering the disparity of the forces. The subsequent concentration of Grant and Hooker with Rosecrans, and the victory of their combined forces at Lookout Mountain, was the result of an audacity or desperation which no military prudence could have foreseen. So confident was Bragg in the impregnability of his position, that immediately after Chickamauga he detached Longstreet, with 16,000 men—about a third of his entire force—to make a demonstration against Knoxville thus indirectly threatening Grant's communications with Nashville. Bragg's position was finally carried by the overwhelming numbers of the enemy. The opponents of his admistration censured Bragg for detaching Longstreet, but the subsequent events which made that movement unfortunate were of a character which no prudence could have foreseen, no military calculation taken into view as probable.

All such reflections were idle, however, concluded Mr. Davis, and he must not be again betrayed into their indulgence. Success is virtue and defeat crime. This is the philosophy of life —at least the only one the great masses of mankind feel ready to accept. Woe to the conquered is no less a popular cry in the nineteenth century than when the barbarians first yelled it as they swarmed with dripping swords to the sack of Rome.

Mr. Davis then spoke of the circumstances attending his flight from Richmond.

On leaving Richmond he went first to Danville, because it was intended that Lee should have moved in that direction, falling back to make a junction with Johnson's force in the direction of Roanoke River. Grant, however, pressed forward so rapidly, and swung so far around, that Lee was obliged to retreat in the direction of Lynchburg with his main force, while his vanguard, which arrived at Danville, insisted on falling back and making the rallying-point at Charlotte in North Carolina.

In Danville Mr. Davis learned of Lee's surrender. Immediately started for Goldsboro', where he met and had a consultation with Gen.

Johnson, thence going on south. At Lexington he received a dispatch from Johnson requesting that the Secretary of War (Gen. Breckinridge) should repair to his headquarters near Raleigh— Gen. Sherman having submitted a proposition for laying down arms which was too comprehensive in its scope for any mere military commander to decide upon. Breckinridge and Postmaster-General Reagan immediately started for Johnson's camp, where Sherman submitted the terms of surrender on which an armistice was declared—the same terms subsequently disapproved by the authorities at Washington.

One of the features of the proposition submitted by General Sherman was a declaration of amnesty to all persons, both civil and military. Notice being called to the fact particularly, Sherman said, "I mean just that"; and gave as his reason that it was the only way to have perfect peace. He had previously offered to furnish a vessel to take away any such persons as Mr. Davis might select, to be freighted with whatever personal property they might want to take with them, and to go wherever it pleased.

General Johnson told Sherman that it was worse

than useless to carry such a proposition as the last to him. Breckinridge also informed General Sherman that his proposition contemplated the adjustment of certain matters which even Mr. Davis was not empowered to control. The terms were accepted, however, with the understanding that they should be liberally construed on both sides, and fulfilled in good faith—General Breckinridge adding that certain parts of the terms would require to be submitted to the various State governments of the Confederacy for ratification.

These terms of agreement between Johnson and Sherman were subsequently disapproved by the authorities at Washington, and the armistice ordered to cease after a certain time. Mr. Davis waited in Charlotte until the day and hour when the armistice ended; then mounted his horse, and, with some cavalry of Duke's brigade (formerly Morgan's), again started southward, passing through South Carolina to Washington, in Georgia. At an encampment on the road, he thinks the cavalry of his escort probably heard of the final surrender of General Johnson, though he himself did not until much later. Being in the advance, he rode on, supposing that the escort was coming after.

As with his party he approached the town of Washington, he was informed that a regiment, supposed to belong to the army of General Thomas, was moving on the place to capture it, in violation, as he thought, of General Sherman's terms. On this he sent back word to the General commanding the cavalry escort to move up and cover the town —an order which probably never reached its destination—at least the cavalry never came; nor did he see them again, nor any of them. Thinking they were coming, however, and not apprehending any molestation from the Federal troops, even if occupying the same town, he entered Washington, and remained there over night—no troops of the United States appearing. Here he heard of his wife and family, not having seen them since they had left Richmond, more than a month before his own departure. They had just left the town before his arrival, moving South in company with his private secretary, Colonel Harrison, of whose fidelity he spoke in warm terms, and accompanied by a small party of paroled men, who, seeing them unprotected, had volunteered to be their escort to Florida, from whence the family, not Mr. Davis himself, intended to take ship to Cuba.

Mr. Davis regarded the section of country he was now in as covered by Sherman's armistice, and had no thought that any expedition could or would be sent for his own capture, or for any other warlike purposes. He believed the terms of Johnson's capitulation still in force over all the country east of the Chattahoochie, which had been embraced in Johnson's immediate command; citing as an evidence of this, that while he was in Washington, General Upton, of the Federal service, with a few members of his staff, passed unattended over the railroad, a few miles from the place, *en route* for Augusta, to receive the muster-rolls of the discharged troops, and take charge of the immense military stores there that fell into General Sherman's hands by the surrender. General Upton was not interfered with, the country being considered at peace, though nothing could have been easier than his capture, had Mr. Davis been so inclined.

At this very time, however, a division of cavalry had been sent into this district, which had been declared at peace and promised exemption from the dangers and burdens of any further military operations within its limits, for the purpose of capturing himself and party; and this he could not but regard as a breach of faith on the part of those who directed or permitted it to be done, though he did not wish to place himself in the condition of one who had accepted the terms of Johnson's capitulation or taken advantage of the amnesty which Sherman had offered. But the district in which he then found himself had been promised exemption from further incursions, and he did not think himself justly liable to capture while within its limits—though he expected to have to take the chances of arrest when once across the Chattahoochie.

Hearing that a skirmish-line, or patrol, had been extended across the country from Macon to Atlanta and thence to Chattanooga, he thought best to go below this line, hoping to join the forces of his relative, Lieutenant General Dick Taylor, after crossing the Chattahoochie. He would then cross the Mississippi, joining Taylor's forces to those of Kirby Smith—of whom he spoke with marked acerbity—and would have continued the fight so long as he could find any Confederate force to strike with him. This, not in any hope of final success, but to secure for the South some better terms than surrender at discretion. "To this complexion," said Mr. Davis, "had the repudiation of General Sherman's terms, and the surrenders of Lee and Johnson, brought the Southern cause."

Mr. Davis left Washington accompanied by Postmaster-General Reagan, three aides, and an escort of ten mounted men with one pack-mule. Riding along, they heard distressing reports of bands of marauders going about the country stealing horses and whatever else might tempt their cupidity—these rumors finally maturing into information which caused him to change his course and follow on to overtake the train containing his wife and family, for whose safety he began to feel apprehensions.

This object he achieved after riding seventy miles, without halt, in a single day, joining Mrs. Davis just at daylight, and in time to prevent a party he had passed on the road from stealing her two fine carriage-horses which formed a particular attraction for their greed. "I have heard," he added, "since my imprisonment, that it was supposed there was a large amount of specie in the train. Such was not the fact, Mrs. Davis carrying with her no money that was not personal property, and but very little of that.''

Having joined his family, he travelled with them for several days, in consequence of finding the region infested with deserters and robbers engaged in plundering whatever was defenceless, his intention being to quit his wife whenever she had reached a safe portion of the country, and to bear west across the Chattahoochie. The very evening before his arrest he was to have carried out this arrangement believing Mrs. Davis to be now safe; but was prevented by a report brought in through one of his aides, that a party of guerillas, or highwaymen, was coming that night to seize the horses and mules of his wife's train. It was on this report he decided to remain another night.

Towards morning he had just fallen into the deep sleep of exhaustion, when his wife's faithful negro servant, Robert, came to him announcing that there was firing up the road. He started up, dressed himself and went out. It was just at grey dawn, and by the imperfect light he saw a party approaching the camp. They were recognised as Federal cavalry by the way in which they deployed to surround the train, and he stepped back into the tent, to warn his wife that the enemy were at hand.

Their tent was prominent, being isolated from the other tents of the train; and as he was quitting it to find his horse, several of the cavalry rode up, directing him to halt and surrender. To this he gave a defiant answer. Then one whom he supposed to be an officer asked, had he any arms, to which Mr. Davis replied: "If I had, you would not be alive to ask that question." His pistols had been left in the holsters, as it had been his intention, the evening before, to start whenever the camp was settled; but horse, saddle, and holsters were now in the enemy's possession, and he was completely unarmed.

Colonel Pritchard, commanding the Federal cavalry, came up soon, to whom Mr. Davis said: "I suppose, sir, your orders are accomplished in arresting me. You can have no wish to interfere with women and children; and I beg they may be permitted to pursue their journey." The Colonel replied that his orders were to take every one found in my company back to Macon, and he would have to do so, though grieved to inconvenience the ladies. Mr. Davis said his wife's party was composed of paroled men, who had committed no act of war since their release, and begged they might be permitted to go to their homes; but the Colonel, under his orders, did not feel at liberty to grant this request. They were all taken to Macon, therefore, reaching it in four days, and from thence were carried by rail to Augusta—Mr. Davis thanking Major-General J. H. Wilson for having treated him with all the courtesy possible to the situation.

The party transferred to Augusta consisted of Reagan, Alexander H. Stevens, Clement C. Clay, two of his own aides and private secretary, Mrs. Clay, his wife and four children, four servants and three paroled men, who had generously offered their protection to Mrs. Davis during her journey. Breckinridge had been with the cavalry brigade, which had been the escort of Mr. Davis, and did not come up at Washington. He and Secretary Benjamin had started for Florida, expecting to escape thence to the West Indies. There was no specie nor public treasure in the train—nothing but his private funds, and of them very little. Some wagons had been furnished by the quartermaster at Washington, Georgia, for the transportation of his family and the paroled men who formed their escort, and that was the only train. Mr. Davis had not seen his family for some months before, and first rejoined them when he rode to their defence from Washington.

June 23d.—I received the following letter from Mrs. Davis:

DATED SAVANNAH, GA., June 14th, 1865.

DR. CRAVEN:

MY DEAR SIR,—Pursued by dreadful pictures thrown before me every day in excerpts from northern correspondents, and published in the daily journals, in which the agony inseparable from defeat and imprisonment is represented to have been heightened for my husband by chains and starvation, I can no longer preserve the silence which I feel should be observed by me, in your failure to answer my letter of the first inst. Can it be that these tales are even in part true? That such atrocities could render him frantic I know is not so. I have so often tended him through months of nervous agony, without ever hearing a groan or an expression of impatience, that I know these tales of childish ravings are not true

—would to God I could believe that all these dreadful rumors were false as well!

But there is something about them which convinces me that they are not altogether false. You must have been kind to him, else he had not told you of his sufferings. Will you not, my dear sir, tell me the worst? Is he ill—is he dying? Taken from me, with only ten minutes' warning, I could not see any one to whom I could say that he was quite ill; indeed, suffering from fever at the hour of our separation. He has been much exposed to a Southern sun in malarial districts, and I dread everything from an attack of illness in his depressed condition, even were the humanities of life manifested to him. With a blaze of light pouring upon the dilated pupils of eyes always sensitive to it; chains fettering his emaciated limbs; coarse food, served, as the newspapers describe it, in the most repulsive manner, without knife, fork, or spoon, "lest he should commit suicide,"—hope seems denied to me; yet I cannot reconcile myself to that result, which for many years must have been his gain. Will you only write me one word to say that he may recover? Will you tell him that we are well—that our little children pray for him, and miss his fatherly care—that his example still lives for them. Please tell him not to be anxious for us; that kind friends are with us, and that those who love him have adopted us, too. Do not tell him, please, that we are not permitted to leave here; for the present, we can do very well, and then I expect, every day, a permit to leave this city for one more healthy. Please try to cheer him about us for we are kindly cared for by the Southern friends who love him here. Will you not take the trouble to write me, only this once? Can it be that you are forbidden? Else, how could a Husband and Father, as I hear you are, refuse us such a small favor, productive as it would be of such blessed comfort?

My children shall pray for you, and perhaps the prayers of "one of these little ones" may avail much with Him who said, "Suffer them to come unto me;" and that which you have done for another may be returned to you with usury in some less happy and prosperous hour. With the hope of hearing from you very soon,

I am, sir,

Very respectfully and gratefully yours,

Varina Davis.

CHAPTER X.

Diseases of the Eye.—Guards removed from the Prisoner's Room.—Mr. Davis takes his first Walk on the Ramparts.—The Policy of Conciliation.—Mr. Davis on Improvements in Land and Naval Warfare.

JUNE 24TH.—Called on Mr. Davis, accompanied by Captain Titlow, Officer of the Day. On entering found the prisoner, for the first time, alone in his cell, the two guards having been removed from it in consequence of my report to Major-General Miles that their presence was counteracting every effort for quieting the nerves of the patient. Mr. Davis remarked that the change had done him good, his last night's sleep having been undisturbed. He complained of his eyes, and a throbbing pain in the back of his neck, asking me to give the matter particular attention, as similar symptoms, at the same season last year, in Richmond, had been followed by a severe bilious remittent fever.

Mr. Davis spoke of the injurious effects of

reflected light upon the eyes, thence diverging to the phenomena of the mirage, and the illusions of vision arising from an over-excited condition of the optic nerve, or peculiar conditions of the atmosphere. The mirage on the deserts of Egypt and Arabia was chiefly observable in the afternoons, when the sands were thoroughly heated, thus producing a different medium of atmosphere close to the earth, and causing the horizontal or vertical refraction, or both, which produced the appearance of this so common phenomenon. Science, he remarked, was fast explaining, as the result of natural laws, nearly all the mysteries of the earth on which ignorance in preceding ages had founded its superstitions and magicians built up a belief in their reputed power. The injurious effects of the whitewash upon the walls of his cell to his eyes, he attributed to the double refractive power—doubly injurious—of all salts and crystallized minerals not retaining the form of the original cube, the regular octohedron, etc.; and of all these substances, the carbonate of lime possessed the double refractive power most eminently, and was, therefore, most injurious to the sight.

Mr. Davis said that reading continually the same type in his Bible and Prayer-Book had become a severe tax upon his sight, of which he had often complained to me before; but what was he to do? Utter inaction for a mind so busy as his had been, was impossible: he must either furnish it with external employment, or allow it to prey upon itself. Nature had furnished all varieties of pabulum to the vision, resting it on one color when weary with another, and changing the forms on which it had been employed with every object of nature. Even with the most healthy, sight was a delicate organ, and with him—the sight of one eye lost and that of the other seriously impaired—peculiarly so. The pupil of the eye was constructed to expand or contract in harmony with each change of light, or color, or different form of object; and to employ the vision continually on one size of type, he believed must be injurious—at least on no other theory could he account for the fast-growing alteration of his sight.

On this subject we had frequently conversed before, my views agreeing with those of Mr. Davis, who, from the necessities of his case, appeared to have pretty thoroughly studied the art of the oculist. Indeed it was a remark which every day impressed on me more forcibly, that the State prisoner had studied no subject superficially, and that his knowledge in all the useful arts and sciences was varied, extensive, and very thorough in each branch.

Representations in regard to the need Mr. Davis stood in of different pabulum, both for his eyes and mind, had been previously made by me to Major-General Miles, and had been confirmed, I rather believe, by Colonel Pineo, Medical Inspector of the Department, who had visited Mr. Davis in my company on the 12th of this month, having a long and interesting conversation with the prisoner—a fact which should have been mentioned at an earlier date; but as the conversation was one in which I took little part, the brief memorandum in my diary escaped notice until revived by the fuller notes of this day's interview. It was upon the day of Colonel Pineo's visit, also, that Mr. Davis mentioned having heard that my little daughter, moved by sympathy, had volunteered as his housekeeper and superintended the sending of his meals. Beautiful as woman's character always was, in its purity, grace, delicacy, and sympathetic action, it was rarely, save in man's hours of deepest affliction, that he realized how much his nature stood in need of the support of his gentle counterpart. Then, picking up a volume of prayer from the table, he said: "Doctor, my wife gave me this. Another, which she placed in my valise, I have since received. Pray present this, with my love and grateful regards, to your little Anna, and say, though I may never have an opportunity to thank her myself, my children will one day rise up 'to call her blessed.'"

And now to have done with this digression and return to my interview of June 24th.

While the State prisoner was yet speaking of the troubles of his sight, Major-General Miles entered, with the pleasant announcement that Mr. Davis was to be allowed to walk one hour each day upon the ramparts, and to have miscellaneous reading hereafter—books, newspapers, and such magazines as might be approved, after perusal at headquarters—an improvement of condition, it must be needless to say, very pleasing to the prisoner.

That afternoon, Mr. Davis took his first walk in the open air since entering Fortress Monroe; Major-General Miles supporting him on one side, the Officer of the Day on the other, and followed by four armed guards. Of this party I was not a member, much to my regret, for the remarks of the prisoner on regaining so much of his liberty, and looking upon scenes formerly so familiar, under happier circumstances, would beyond doubt have been of interest. I only noticed that Mr. Davis was arrayed in the same garb he had worn when entering his cell—indeed General Miles had possession of all his other wardrobe; and that while his carriage was proud and erect as ever, not losing a hair's breadth of his height from any stoop, his step had lost its elasticity, his gait was feeble in the extreme, and he had frequently to press his chest, panting in the pauses of exertion. The cortege promenaded along the ramparts of the South front, Mr. Davis often stopping and pointing out objects of interest, as if giving reminiscences of the past and making inquiries of the present. He was so weak, however, that the hour allowed proved nearly twice too much for him, and he had to be led back with only half his offered liberty enjoyed.

June 25th.—Visited prisoner with Captain Evans, 3d Pennsylvania Artillery, Officer of the Day. Mr. Davis much better, and with spirits greatly improved. The application to the back of his neck had immediately relieved the pain, and his sight was less wavering. He no longer saw the cloud of black and amber motes rising and falling before his sight. The nervous and painful twitching of the eyelids had also in great measure ceased. Of all diseases, he most feared photophobia, having seen many cases of it, and heard it was the keenest agony of which the human nerves are susceptible. Injured as his sight was, he knew such a disease must result in total blindness. "Not that I expect many pleasant things to look out upon, Doctor, but that I need my sight for my defence, which must also be the defence of the cause I represented, and which my sufferings have been aimed to degrade."

Asked him how he had enjoyed his walk on the previous afternoon. He said the sense of breathing air not drawn through iron bars was a glorious blessing, only to be appreciated by prisoners—one of the thousand common blessings which must be lost before we prize them. The varieties

of view and animation of the scene had stimulated
and reinvigorated his eyes; but his feebleness had
been excessive—partly arising, he thought, from a
rush of novel emotions, partly from the old recollections that came crowding back to him; and
partly because, looking towards the land of his
people from the Southern front, it seemed to his
mind a vast charnel-house, with the black plumes
of political death nodding between it and the sun.

"And yet this should not be," continued Mr.
Davis, "if your authorities at Washington be
wise. The attempt of certain States to separate
from the old confederation, in which their rights
under the fundamental law had been violated,
having proved abortive, and they being coerced
back under the General Government by military
force, their rights under the Constitution at once
return, and revive with their submission, unless
that instrument shall be deliberately and openly
repudiated. Such was the absolute spirit of
General Grant's negotiation upon which General
Lee surrendered; and such both the spirit and
letter of General Sherman's proposals to the General he was contending against (General Johnson's
name not mentioned). "It was also embodied

in all the declarations of your Government and late President in all their public acts; and I think my people would have fought more desperately, and continued the war much longer, though hopelessly, had it not been for this expectation.

"But even apart from this—apart from all pledges of faith or obligations of constitutional law," Mr. Davis went on, "and looking on the matter only in the light of future expediency, let us see how the case stands. In the better days of the Roman empire, when its possessions increased, and conquered countries came in a few years to be integral, and even zealous members of the imperial system, it was the policy of conciliation, following that of military conquest, which achieved the desired results. Certain laws and restrictions of the imperial government were imposed—so much annual tribute, so many legions to our military levies, and obedience to all such laws of the Central Government as may be issued for your control. But within these lines, and with these points conceded the empire strove in all minor and domestic matters to conform, in so far as might be possible, to the former habits, customs, and laws of the people absorbed, and the independent governments superseded. Even their peculiarities of morals, manners, and religious views were studied and respected, when not conflicting with the necessities of the empire; their leading men were justly treated, and no efforts were spared to make the new order of things sit lightly at first, and even pleasantly in a few years, on the necks of the subjugated provinces. Generosity is the true policy, both of nations and individuals. 'There is that maketh himself rich, yet hath nothing; there is that maketh himself poor, yet hath great riches.' While my people are held as conquered subjects, they must be to you a continued source of expense and danger—a country penned together with bayonets. Let the past be expunged, if you please; we have nothing to blush for in it, and nothing to regret but failure. The necessities of the Northern treasury and public debt," Mr. Davis thought, "would, before long, compel us to do justice to this section."

Mr. Davis then spoke of the immense improvements in the art and practice of war which the recent struggle had developed; this in connection with the progress of work on the Rip Raps, some iron-clads he had seen in the roadstead, and the fifteen-inch Rodman guns which now stand *en barbette* on each bastion of the fort.

England's naval supremacy he considered lost by the invention of iron-clads, these converting the conditions of maritime warfare from a question of dexterity and *personnel* into one of machinery and in machinery the Americans could have no superiors, while in all other qualities they were at least the equals of the British. The science of naval gunnery had also been revolutionized, the new principle being to concentrate into a single crushing shot the former scattered forces of a broadside. The problem of the iron-clad was to attain the maximum of offensive power while exposing the least possible and most strongly armored objective points to the projectiles of the enemy; and in such plans of our iron-clads as he had lately seen, these desiderata seemed to have been very nearly attained. For crossing the ocean, however, and for cruising on peaceful stations, our vessels lay too low in the water, either for safety from storms, or the comfort and health of the crews and officers. If our present vessels had in them vast wells, which, when empty, would cause the hulls to float eight or ten feet above the water, and which, on being filled when going into action, would reduce them to their present level, he thought no grander instruments of belligerency could be imagined. Wooden bottoms, with armored sides and armored turrets, he could not but think would prove the best. The enormous weight superimposed, coupled with the rollings of the sea, must soon chafe and wear away the rivets and plates of an iron bottom, no matter how carefully secured; while wooden hulls sat more easily on the water, and both avoided chafing and obtained greater speed by their capacity of yielding a little. Even the sea in its laws, concluded Mr. Davis with a smile, teaches the policy of conciliation—of concession; vessels making headway as their lines conform to the resistence of the ocean, and have some power of yielding to the pressure of the billows. To attain the greatest speed, we should take for a model the swiftest fish, and conform to that as much as circumstances would permit; and in this connection he referred approvingly to the cigar-shaped vessels of Mr. Winans, of Baltimore.

In regard to the improvements in ordnance,

he spoke at great length, displaying not merely a very observant knowledge of all the changes in modern artillery and projectiles, but also of the science of metallurgy as applied to the production of ordnance. He discussed the atomic theory, or relationship of particles, and the effects on iron fibre of different temperatures and treatments, as by hammering, rolling, and the various methods of cooling; detailing with a minuteness I could not hope to follow, numerous experiments in the construction and effect of ordnance while he was Secretary of War. The Swedish and Russian iron had been reputed best, but he thought experiment would prove that the iron of the Shenandoah Valley and of Eastern Tennessee, when properly treated, would be at least as good, if not superior, for this climate. In the Tredegar Iron-Works, an enormous amount of work had been done, and many improvements in puddling and casting introduced; but the continued and ever-increasing necessities of the war, as the blockade became more effective, made rapidity the one thing needful, and much of the work, more especially of late, had been rough and defective.

Rifled guns he had been at first inclined to

favor, and for certain classes of service at long range, they must always remain the best. For tearing and destroying forts of masonry, the results at Pulaski and Sumter had demonstrated their value; but as earthworks would hereafter be employed wherever possible, their superiority in this respect was of less importance. For naval engagements, at long range, they would also be better; but with iron-clad ships, all future engagements must be within a few hundred yards, and then the slow, crushing shot of the heavy smooth bore was the thing needed. For chasing a blockade-runner or crippling a flying ship, the rifled gun; but for crushing in the sides or turret of an armored vessel, the heavy thirteen or fifteen-inch shot from a smooth bore, propelled by slow-burning powder, would be most efficacious. Quick-burning powder strained the gun too much by its shock, hurled out the projectile before the powder behind it had been half developed, and also wasted not less than a third of the charge before the process of combustion had time to take place. He spoke of Captain Dahlgren and his experiments in ordnance while he (Mr. Davis) had been Secretary of War, remarking that, rightly or wrongly, the Captain had been accused of appropriating as his own, with very trivial alterations, if any, discoveries which were submitted to him for examination and report as chief of ordnance in the navy yard. Of the Rodman he spoke approvingly, regarding its chilling process as the true one; but for perfection of elaborate workmanship and detail no guns he had ever seen were superior to some of those received through the blockade from England. It was a mistake, however, to be too minute in war. War was a rough business, and rough tools would carry it through if there were only plenty of them, and in the hands of anything like a sufficiency of proper men.

From this time, the prisoner received books and newspapers freely, chiefly reading of newspapers, the *New York Herald*, and of books, histories—Mr. Bancroft appearing his favorite American author. I recommended him to be very moderate at first in his open-air exercise, gauging the amount of exercise to his strength; and from this time forward Mr. Davis went out every day for an hour's exercise, the weather and his health permitting.

CHAPTER XI.

*Mr. Lincoln's Assassination.—Ex-President Pierce.
—Torture of being Constantly Watched.—Mr.
Davis on the Members of his Cabinet and the
Opponents of his Administration.—Touching
Tribute to the Memory of "Stonewall" Jackson.*

SUNDAY, JULY 11TH.—Was sent for by Mr. Davis,
and called in company with Captain R. O. Bickley,
Officer of the Day.

Found prisoner very desponding, the failure
of his sight troubling him, and his nights almost
without sleep. His present treatment was killing
him by inches, and he wished shorter work could
be made of his torment. He had hoped long
since for a trial, which should be public, and
therefore with some semblance of fairness; but
hope deferred was making his heart sick. The
odious, malignant and absurd insinuation that he
was connected in some manner with the great
crime and folly of Mr. Lincoln's assassination,
was his chief personal motive for so earnestly

147

desiring an early opportunity of vindication.
But apart from this, as he was evidently made the
representative in whose person the action of the
seceding States was to be argued and decided,
he yet more strongly desired for this reason to be
heard in behalf of the defeated, but to him still
sacred cause. The defeat he accepted, as a man
has to accept all necessities of accomplished fact;
but to vindicate the theory and justice of his
cause, showing by the authority of the Constitution and the Fathers of the Country, that his people
had only asserted a right—had committed no
crime; this was the last remaining labor which
life could impose on him as a public duty. Mr.
Davis then spoke of Ex-President Franklin Pierce
in terms of warm admiration, as the public man
who had studied constitutional law, and the relation of the States to highest profit, remarking,
that if he were given any choice of counsel, Mr.
Pierce would be one of those whose advice he
would think most reliable. He also spoke of Mr.
Charles Eames, of Washington, as a walking
encyclopædia of constitutional law, very accurate
and ready in his reference to precedents; adding
that he had seen a report in the *Herald* that Messrs.

Reverdy Johnson, of Maryland, and Charles O'Conor, of New York, had professed their readiness to assume his defence, when approached by some of his friends for that purpose, for which he felt grateful, both personally and for his people. His own fate was of no importance in this matter, save to the Government, on which history would devolve the responsibility for his treatment. Martyrdom, while representing the deliberate action of his people, would be immortality; but for the sake of justice, not merely to his own people, but to the whole American people, whose future liberties were now at stake in his person, a fair and public trial was now the necessity of the situation.

"My people," he added, "attempted what your people denounced as a revolution. My people failed, but your people have suffered a revolution which must prove disastrous to their liberties unless promptly remedied by legal decision, in their efforts to resist the revolution which they charged my people with contemplating. State sovereignty, the corner-stone of the Constitution, has become a name. There is no longer power, or will, in any State, or number of States, that would dare refuse compliance with any tinkle of Mr. Seward's bell."

Mr. Davis complained his sleeplessness was aggravated by the lamp kept burning in his room all night, so that he could be seen at all moments by the guard in the outer cell. If he happened to doze one feverish moment, the noise of relieving guard in the next room aroused him, and the lamp poured its full glare into his aching and throbbing eyes. There must be a change in this, or he would go crazy, or blind, or both.

"Doctor," he said, "had you ever the consciousness of being watched? Of having an eye fixed on you every moment, intently scrutinizing your most minute actions, and the variations of your countenance and posture? The consciousness that the Omniscient Eye rests upon us, in every situation, is the most consoling and beautiful belief of religion. But to have a human eye riveted on you in every moment of waking or sleeping, sitting, walking, or lying down, is a refinement of torture on anything the Comanches or Spanish Inquisition ever dreamed. They, in their ignorance of cruel art, only struck at the body; and the nerves have a very limited capacity of pain.

This is a maddening, incessant torture of the mind, increasing with every moment it is endured, and shaking the reason by its incessant recurrence of miserable pain. Letting a single drop of water fall on the head every sixty seconds does not hurt at first, but its victim dies of raving agony, it is alleged, if the infliction be continued. The torture of being incessantly watched is, to the mind, what the water-dropping is to the body, but more afflictive, as the mind is more susceptible of pain. The Eye of Omniscience looks upon us with tenderness and compassion; even if conscious of guilt, we have the comfort of knowing that Eye sees also our repentance. But the human eye forever fixed upon you is the eye of a spy, or enemy, gloating in the pain and humiliation which itself creates. I have lived too long in the woods to be frightened by an owl, and have seen death too often to dread any form of pain. But I confess, Doctor, this torture of being watched begins to prey on my reason. The lamp burning in my room all night would seem a torment devised by some one who had intimate knowledge of my habits, my custom having been through life never to sleep except in total darkness."

This conversation, so far as related to its medical aspect, I deemed it my duty to communicate that afternoon to Major-General Miles, who could not remove the lamp altogether, but directed that it should be screened at night, so that no direct and glaring beams should be thrown into the prisoner's eyes.

Soon after this interview, I received a third letter from Mrs. Davis, as follows:

SAVANNAH, GA., July 2, 1865.

DR. J. J. CRAVEN:

MY DEAR SIR,—I have written to you three times, and no answer has been returned; but I am not capable of the "still yet brave despair," which I know is required in my hopeless position. Thanks to God, that He has raised you up a "present help" in my husband's time of trouble, are daily rendered.

Am I intrusive in offering gratitude and earnest prayers for your welfare and that of your household, and for your manly disregard of everything but the suffering man before you? I know you have been kind, for the only concordance between any of the numberless harrowing statements which daily agonize me, is that you are always represented as kind to him—as ministering to his necessity. The last account tells me that your wife and little daughter are also kind enough to attend to his wants. With my gratitude and joy that even in such a dungeon, separated from all his earthly ties he is not alone, comes the sad memory that I can do nothing but write to say how I love them for their goodness; how I long to see their faces before my eyes are closed in death! I am not alone in offering to them loving thanks—our whole people join me in offering acknowledgments to them and to you. Many little children, besides my own poor little ones, have asked me if I had a likeness of your family, that they might form an idea of those whose kindness has become to them household words. Still no word of comforting response comes to me from you. I will not annoy you by importunities; but pray that we may meet at some future day, when such painful circumstances as now surround me may have been swept away by God's christianizing grace.

When "martial faith and courtesy" may again dictate the action of those who now hold my suffering husband "a prisoner of war," but treat him like a felon, a heart full of gratitude, over-flowing in earnest, constant prayers for you, and for your dear wife, and little Annie, is all I have to offer; and these are ever present to

Yours most gratefully,

VARINA DAVIS.

July 15th.—Called on Mr. Davis, accompanied by Captain Grill, 3d Pennsylvania Artillery, Officer of the Day. Found him extremely weak, and growing more alarmed about his sight, which was failing rapidly. The phenomenon had occurred to him of seeing all objects double, due chiefly to his nervous debility and the over-taxation of constant reading. Prescribed stimulants internally—weak brandy and water with his meals to aid digestion—and a stimulating wash.

Some remarks he had seen in one of the New York papers led Mr. Davis to speak of the difficulties which had surrounded his administration.

His Cabinet had been selected during the formation of the Provisional Government at Montgomery when there were but seven States in the Confederacy from which to select or accept Secretaries, and when all things were in dire confusion—even those of farthest sight in public affairs with but little prevision of what lay before them. Georgia, as the largest State represented in the Provisional Congress, claimed the portfolio of State and recommended Mr. Toombs—a man of great natural force and capacity, but a destroyer, not a builder up; a man of restless nature, a born Jacobin, though with honest intentions. Alabama, as the second State, claimed the portfolio of War, and nominated Pope Walker for the position—a gentleman of excellent intentions, but wholly without the requisite experience or capacities for so vast a trust. South Carolina placed Mr. Memminger in the Treasury, and while he respected the man, the utter failure of Confederate finance was the failure of the cause. Had Mr. Memminger acted promptly on the proposition of depositing cotton in Europe and holding it there for two years as a basis for their currency, their circulating medium might have maintained itself at par to the closing day of the struggle; and that in itself would have insured victory. Louisiana sent Benjamin, the ablest and most faithful member of his advisory council; a man who realized that industry is the mistress of success, and who had no personal aspirations, no wishes that were not subordinate to the prosperity of the cause. In the early part of the war, Benjamin furnished a parallel to Mr. Seward, both believing and avowing that the impending crisis would not last longer than sixty or ninety days, though Benjamin relaxed no labor or preparation on that account. Texas had the Postal Department in the person of Mr. Reagan, who was a plain, strong man, of good common sense and a good heart, faithful to the cause with zealous fidelity, and faithful to the last, though endowed with no peculiar administrative abilities, and one of those who had not labored to precipitate secession, though accepting it heartily as a political necessity when it came. The Navy Department went to Florida, and was filled by Mr. Mallory, who had large experience in the Naval Committee of the United States Senate. It was complained that there had been remissness in this department, no Confederate war vessel having been commenced until eight or nine months after the act of secession. In these complaints there was doubtless some truth; but after an event happened, prophesying was cheap. No one at that day could have foreseen the extent or prolongation of the struggle, and the belief was common, if not natural, that the necessities of Europe would compel foreign nations to raise the blockade, and finally bring the naval resources of England and France to the aid of his people.

Being interested by what Mr. Davis said of the failure of the Confederate currency as the failure of the cause, and of some scheme by which it might have been prevented, I expressed my curiosity and ventured to request some explanation, as there appeared to me no manner in which Confederate paper could have been sustained at par.

Mr. Davis replied that one rule of his life was, never to express regret for the inevitable: to let the dead bury its dead in regard to all political hopes that were not realized. Fire is not quenched with tow, nor the past to be remedied by lamentations. It would, however, have been possible, in his judgment, to have kept the currency of his people good for gold, or very nearly so, during the entire struggle; and had this been done, the contrast, if nothing else, would have reduced United States securities to zero, and so terminated the contest. The plan urged upon Mr. Memminger was as follows—a plan Mr. Davis privately approved, but had not time to study and take the responsibility of directing, until too late:—

At the time of secession there were not less than three million bales of cotton in the South—plantation bales, of 400 pounds weight each. These the Secretary of the Treasury recommended to buy from the planters, who were then willing, and even eager, to sell to the government, at ten cents per pound of Confederate currency. These three million bales were to be rushed off to Europe before the blockade was of any efficiency, and there held for one or two years, until the price reached not less than 70 or 80 cents per pound— and we all know it reached much higher during the war. This would have given a cash basis in Europe of not less than a thousand million dollars in gold, and all securities drawn against this balance in bank would maintain par value. Such a sum would have more than sufficed all the needs of the Confederacy during the war; would have sufficed, with economic management, for a war of twice the actual duration; and this evidence of Southern prosperity and stability could not but have acted powerfully on the minds, the securities and the avarice of the New England rulers of the North. He was far from reproaching Mr. Memminger. The situation was new. No one could have foreseen the course of events. When too late the wisdom of the proposed measure was realized, but the inevitable "too late" was interposed. The blockade had become too stringent, for one reason, and the planters had lost their pristine confidence in Confederate currency. When we might have put silver in the purse, we did not put it there. When we had only silver on the tongue, our promises were forced to become excessive.

I asked how Mr. Memminger had obtained prominence in so aristocratic a State as South Carolina, the report being that he was a foundling born with little claim to either wealth or name. Mr. Davis said he knew nothing of the matter, and immediately turned away the conversation, appearing displeased.

When Mr. Benjamin was made Secretary of War, Mr. Davis continued—Mr. Walker having proved a failure—Congress was pleased to blame him for the successes of General Burnside at Roanoke Island, and so forth; events which no human activity or foresight, with the forces at his command, could have averted. Congress in some respects was slow to provide against reverses, but never lacking in promptness to find a scapegoat. From the first, there was a strong party in in the South—or rather in the Southern Congress and political life—arrayed against his administration. They never deemed it wise to attack him personally or directly, for his people were devotedly and nobly faithful to the representative of their selection; but the plan was to assail any man or measure in whom or which Mr. Davis was supposed—often erroneously—to take special interest. He himself was much to blame for this, perhaps— his fidelity to friendship and the natural combativeness of his nature, prompting him to assume as personal to himself, any assaults directed against men or measures for whose appointment or origination he was in any degree responsible. This was a fault of his temperament, but each man must accept himself as he stands, and that man does well who makes out of himself the best possible.

Toombs, even when in the Cabinet, had been impracticable and restless. Out of it he became an active malcontent, and was powerfully supported in every perverse and pernicious suggestion by Governor Brown, of Georgia. Vice-President Stephens had lent the government no assistance, continually holding himself aloof from Richmond —perhaps on account of ill health; but certainly his health must have been very wretched indeed, if poorer than that of Mr. Davis, during many of his most trying and laborious months. Be the cause what it might, however, the absence, if not apathy, of Mr. Stephens, had been an element of weakness, and led him to be regarded by the malcontents as a friend and pillar of their cause. In South Carolina, there was the Rhett faction; never at home save when in the attitude of contradiction; men whose lives were expended in the negative, and who often recalled to his mind the contradictory gentleman described by Sydney Smith, who, when he had no one else to quarrel with, threw up his window at night for the purpose of contradicting the watchman who was shouting, "Two o'clock—all well." The only open assailant he had in Congress was Senator Foote, of his own State—a man of no account or credit; an inveterate place-hunter and mere politician, who appeared laboring under a constitutional inability either to see anything correctly, or to report correctly what he had seen.

Of Stonewall Jackson, Mr. Davis spoke with the utmost tenderness, and some touch of reverential feeling, bearing witness to his earnest and pathetic piety, his singleness of aim, his immense energy as an executive officer, and the loyalty of his nature, making obedience the first of all duties. "He rose every morning at three," said Mr. Davis; "performed his devotions for half an hour, and then went booming along at the head of his command, which came to be called 'Jackson's foot cavalry,' from the velocity of their movements. He had the faculty, or rather gift, of exciting and holding the love and confidence of his men to an unbounded degree, even though the character of his campaigning imposed on them more hardships than on any other troops in the service. Good soldiers care not for their individual sacrifices when adequate results can be shown; and these General Jackson never lacked. Hard fighting, hard marching, hard fare, the strictest discipline —all these men will bear, if visibly approaching the goal of their hopes. They want to get done with the war, back to their homes and families; and their instinct soon teaches them which commander is pursuing the right means to accomplish these results. Jackson was a singularly ungainly man on horseback, and had many peculiarities of temper, amounting to violent idiosyncrasies; but everything in his nature, though here and there uncouth, was noble. Even in the heat of action, and when most exposed, he might be seen throwing up his hands in prayer. For glory he lived long enough," continued Mr. Davis with much emotion; "and if this result had to come, it was the Divine mercy that removed him. He fell like the eagle, his own feather on the shaft that was dripping with his life-blood. In his death the Confederacy lost an eye and arm, our only consolation being that the final summons could have reached no soldier more prepared to accept it joyfully. Jackson was not of a sanguine turn, always privately anticipating the worst, that the better might be more welcome."

CHAPTER XII.

Mr. Davis seriously Ill.—Restrictions on Corres-
pondence with his Wife.—Clement C. Clay.—A
Rampart Interview.—Religious Phase of Mr.
Davis's Character.

JULY 20TH.—Called on Mr. Davis, Captain Korte, 3d Pennsylvania Artillery, being Officer of the Day, and, of course, my companion. Was requested to call by Major-General Miles, who had received report that prisoner was seriously ill.

Found Mr. Davis in a very critical state; his nervous debility extreme; his mind more despondent than ever heretofore; his appetite gone; complexion livid, and pulse denoting deep prostration of all the physical energies. Was much alarmed, and realized with painful anxiety the responsibilities of my position. If he were to die in prison, and without trial, subject to such severities as had been inflicted on his attenuated frame, the world would form unjust conclusions, but conclusions with enough color to pass them into history. It seemed to me, let me frankly confess, due to the honor of America, and the future glory of our struggle for national existence, that this result should not happen.

Mr. Davis asked me could nothing be done to better his condition, or secure him the justice of a trial before death. The effort of his people to establish a country had failed, and they had no country now but America. It was for the honor of America, not less than for his own, and for justice to his cause, that he pleaded.

Assured Mr. Davis that no effort of care or such skill as I possessed should be wanting for his benefit. Then commenced conversation on various topics, seeking to divert his mind from the afflictions preying on it.

Talking of the Confederate flag and the various flags under which the regiments of each State fought, I mentioned having once seen a curious practical realization of the flag of South Carolina —the palmetto-tree and rattlesnake.

The day after the success of Admiral Du Pont at Port Royal, and the landing of Sherman's expedition on Hilton Head, I had ridden out in company with General Horatio G. Wright to an abandoned cavalry camp of the expelled troops. There, twisted around the trunk of a palmetto-tree, and held in his place round it by ligatures of reeds, was a dead rattlesnake, the largest I had ever seen, some eight feet long, and probably nearly a hundred pounds weight. It had undoubtedly been placed there in sport by some of the cavalry as an emblem of the flag of their State.

"It was a good omen for you," said Mr. Davis, with a faint smile, and then commenced talking of the snakes of the Southern coast. He mentioned as curious that the deer, usually the most timid of animals, or so popularly regarded, was the deadliest enemy of the rattlesnake. Wherever and whenever finding one in the woods near the coast, or on the grassy sand-heaps which the snake so loved, the deer commenced assailing it acrimoniously with its sharp and powerful though dainty fore-hoofs. These it would jab or dig into the rattlesnake's head, half stunning it the first blow. Then the deer would graze a few moments—with a wary eye on the snake, however, repeating its stabs with its sharp hoofs until its enemy expired. The negroes accounted for the immunity of the deer in these encounters by the fact that its delicate forelegs, being nearly all skin and bone, were the only parts exposed within reach of the rattlesnake, and had too little blood or flesh in them to convey the virus. It was not true that this snake could project himself the full length of his coil. He could only coil up half his length and throw that forward. They are slow and of little danger to men or dogs, unless suddenly trodden upon. No instance of their attacking a man, unless attacked, was on record along the Southern coast. They like the cool sea-breezes, and feed on rabbits and squirrels, which they have great dexterity in catching. Mr. Davis had never heard of any specific cure for their bite save when the part could be instantly amputated before the poison spread. Powerful doses of whiskey were a remedy in some cases—perhaps on the principle of the more powerful poison expelling the weaker. He had known a case, when serving on the frontier, in which this remedy had proved worse than the disease. A very worthy sergeant of the 1st Dragoons had been formerly of intemperate habits, but had reformed and been perfectly abstemious for several years. Some kind of a snake bit him —probably one whose bite was not mortal, though painful—and heavy doses of whiskey were at once prescribed. This re-aroused the slumbering devil, and in less than six months after the sergeant, degraded to the ranks, died of *mania a potu* in the guard-house. Drunkenness is the great vice of soldiers, and worked much misery with his people. The social glass, carried to excess, becomes a pair of spectacles through which men gaze into the bottomless pit. Mr. Davis then referred jocosely to the old form of commissary requisitions for whiskey when he was in the army: "So many barrels of whiskey to cure snake-bites." This was because whiskey was forbidden in army stores, unless to be used for medicinal purposes. He believed ten thousand soldiers had "seen snakes," as the phrase ran, through this agency, for the one who had been cured of a snake-bite.

The moccasin-snake, which is also very poisonous —though not so deadly on the southern coast-line as in the interior—seldom grows to be over three feet in length, and is thicker and slower of motion than the rattlesnake. The chicken or house-snake often grows to great size, fully as large as the rattle-snake, but is not dangerously poisonous, though its fangs create an unpleasant pustule, death occasionally resulting when they happen to pierce a vein. They are swift, feed on birds and poultry of all kinds, and have greater power of convolution and contortion than any other snakes, this being necessary to enable them to climb trees in pursuit of their prey with the requisite quickness. Children often attacked these snakes when finding them curled up in the crevices of barns or abandoned houses, rarely failing to kill them. The moccasin-snake is rather more omnivorous than the others, feeding upon frogs, toads, birds, beetles, rabbits, or whatever it can catch.

Mr. Davis said when he had last been out on the ramparts he had met Mr. C. C. Clay, similarly walking under guard. Clay was looking wretchedly and seeing him made Mr. Davis realize more acutely his own humiliating position. Men at sea in a ship never realize how forlorn and frail the vessel is they are on board, until their counterpart in some closely passing vessel is brought under notice. Absorbed in exercise and the emotions of the scene, he had previously failed to realize his situation, with an officer at his side as custodian, and four bayonets pacing behind him to secure that he should make no effort to escape. The moment

Mr. Clay passed, his own situation stood revealed; and nothing but his strong conviction that to remain in his cell would be equivalent to suicide, could induce him to parade again in the same manner. As he passed Mr. Clay, they exchanged a few words in French, nothing more than the compliments of the day and an inquiry for each other's health; but it seemed this had alarmed the officer, who did not understand the language, Mr. Clay not being permitted to pass him again, but being marched off to another part of the ramparts. Clay was naturally delicate, of an atrabilious type, and his appearance denoted that he must be suffering severely.

Replied that I had been attending Mr. Clay, and saw nothing in his state to occasion alarm. He had a tendency to asthma, but that was a long-lived disease. Mr. Davis inquired how Clay was fed. Replied that at first he had received soldier's rations, but latterly, his condition demanding it, had been fed from the hospital. Mr. Davis expressed much sympathy for his fellow-sufferer, begging me to do whatever I professionally could for his relief, and to hold up his hands. Let me here remark that, despite a certain exterior

cynicism of manner, no patient has ever crossed
my path, who, suffering so much himself, appeared
to feel so warmly and tenderly for others. Sickness, as a general rule, is sadly selfish; its own
pains and infirmities occupying too much of its
thoughts. With Mr. Davis, however, the rule did
not work, or rather he was an exception calling
attention to its general truth.

Prisoner complained bitterly of the restrictions
imposed by General Miles on his correspondence
with his wife; certain subjects, and those perhaps
of most interest, being forbidden to both. The
convicts in State prisons were allowed this liberty
unimpeded, or only subject to the supervision of
the Chaplain, whose scrutiny had a religious and
kindly character—that of a Father Confessor.
His letters, on the contrary, had to be sent open
to General Miles, and from him, he understood,
similarly open to the Attorney-General. What
unbosoming of confidence—mutual griefs, mutual
hopes, the interchange of tenderest sympathies
—was possible, or would be delicate under such
a system! He pictured idle young staff-officers
here, or yet more pitiful clerks in the Law Department at Washington, grinning over any confessions

of pain, or terms of endearment, he might be tempted to use; and this thought embittered the pleasure such correspondence might otherwise have conferred. The relationship of husband and wife was the inner vestibule of the temple—the holy of holies—in poor human life; and who could expose its secrets, or lay his heart bare on his sleeve, for such daws to peck at? Even criminals condemned to death for heinous crimes, were allowed not only free correspondence with their wives, but interviews at which no jailer stood within earshot. What possible public danger could there be from allowing such letters to pass without scrutiny? Time will set all these petty tyrannies in their true light. He that first pleadeth his own cause seems justified; but his neighbor cometh and searcheth him. If the privilege were ever abused—if anything he wrote to his wife were published to the detriment of the government, or tending to disturb the peace, what easier than to say, "This privilege has been abused, and must cease?"

July 21st.—Visited prisoner with Captain Evans, 3d Pennsylvania Artillery, Officer of the Day. Mr. Davis better, but still in bed; the Bible and

Prayer-Book his usual companions. Complained that his irritation of sight made reading painful; but there was consolation for greater sacrifice in what he read.

There was no affectation of devoutness or ascetism in my patient; but every opportunity I had of seeing him, convinced me more deeply of his sincere religious convictions. He was fond of referring to passages of Scripture, comparing text with text; dwelling on the divine beauty of the imagery, and the wonderful adaptation of the whole to every conceivable phase and stage of human life. Nothing that any man's individual experience, however strange, could bring home to him, but had been previously foretold and described, with its proper lesson or promise of hope, in the sacred volume. It was the only absolute wisdom, reaching all varieties of existence, because comprehending the whole; and, besides its inspired universal knowledge, all the learning of humanity was but foolishness. The Psalms were his favorite portion of the Word, and had always been. Evidence of their divine origin was inherent in their text. Only an intelligence that held the life-threads of the entire human family could have thus pealed forth in a single cry every wish, joy, fear, exultation, hope, passion, and sorrow of the human heart. There were moments, while speaking on religious subjects, in which Mr. Davis impressed me more than any professor of Christianity I had ever heard. There was a vital earnestness in his discourse; a clear, almost passionate grasp in his faith; and the thought would frequently recur, that a belief capable of consoling such sorrows as his, possessed, and hereby evidenced, a reality—a substance—which no sophistry of the infidel could discredit.

To this phase of the prisoner's character I have heretofore rather avoided calling attention for several reasons, prominent of which, though an unworthy one, was this: My knowledge that many, if not a majority of my readers, would approach the character of Mr. Davis with a preconception of dislike and distrust, and a consequent fear that an earlier forcing on their attention of this phase of his character, before their opinion had been modified by such glimpses as are herein given, might only challenge a base and false imputation of hypocrisy against one than whom, in my judgment, no more devout exemplar of Christian faith, and its value as a consolation, now lives, whatever may have been his political crimes or errors.

And here, dropping the note-book a moment, let me say a few words in my own character— a reflection continually brought to my notice by each day's further acquaintance with Mr. Davis:

Is it not true that the chief mistakes and prejudices of public opinion come from our not understanding—not seeking to understand—the true motives and characters of the men to whom we are opposed? Blind and hot-headed partisanship, speaking in the haste of the press and the heat of the rostrum, accepts without evidence whatever epithet of infamy can be applied to the object of its dislike; no stories of guilt or folly that can degrade or render hateful the foeman we stand arrayed against, can be too monstrous to find believers, at least while the struggle lasts. But in a few years, as we recede from the convulsed and frenzied period of the strife, we grow to be ashamed of the malignant delusions which have so grossly cheated our senses; and before history takes up the pen to record her final judgment, the world will be willing to concede that the man was not utterly bad—had, in fact, great redeeming virtues—who was our most prominent foe; and that no movement so vast, and eliciting such intense devotion on the part of its partisans as the late Southern rebellion, could have grown up into its gigantic proportions without containing many elements of truth and good, which it may profit future ages to study attentively, though the means taken for the assertion of its principles were false, criminal, and only fraught with disaster.

To anticipate a little what must be the inevitable course of events, to give the public such opportunity as was given the writer of judging Jefferson Davis from a clearer standpoint, and to save the present generation of the North from the fatal error of continuing to regard and treat as a common criminal the chief actor opposed to us in a struggle the most gigantic the world has ever seen, and with which history will ring for centuries to come —if these objects can be attained, the author will not have toiled in vain. All the crimes that an evil ingenuity has yet been able to impute to this man, are as new-fallen snow when brought in contrast with the fabrications of the English and

European press in regard to the murderous and incestuous proclivities of the first Napoleon during the great wars in which that Captain involved the elder continent. But such is not now the judgment of him, either in England or in the world's history—nor will history consent to regard Mr. Davis in the odious, monstrous, or contemptible light which has been, for the last five years, the only one in which the necessities and passions of our recent struggle would permit him to be presented to our gaze.

CHAPTER XIII.

Southern Migration to Mexico.—Mr. Calhoun's Memory vindicated from one Charge.—Tribute to Albert Sidney Johnston.—Failure of Southern Iron-clads and Loss of the Mississippi.

JULY 24TH.—Called on Mr. Davis, accompanied by Captain Korte, 3d Pennsylvania Artillery, Officer of the Day. Found prisoner still very feeble, but said he could not resist the temptation to crawl out in such beautiful weather, even at the cost of the degrading guards who dogged his steps. Captain Korte absent during greater part of this interview, relieving guard in the casemates of Clay and other prisoners. Some officers of the day often left me alone with prisoner for this purpose; others remained close to us as we conversed; but as Mr. Davis always spoke in a subdued manner, and my replies were given in the usual confidential tone of a doctor consulting a patient, the presence or absence of the Officer of the Day made little difference.

178

Mr. Davis spoke of the folly and something worse of those Southern leaders who had fled to Mexico. It was an act of cowardice—an evasion of duty only to be excelled by suicide. They had been instrumental in bringing the evils of military subjugation on the people, and should remain to share their burdens. The great masses of the people were rooted to the soil, and could not, and should not, fly. The first duty of the men who had been in command during the struggle was, to remain faithful fellow-sufferers with the rank and file. By doing so they could yet exercise a moral and intellectual, if not political, weight against the schemers of rapine and oppression now swarming over the Southern country; while by deserting, they abandon helpless ignorance to the sway of powerful craft, and confessed judgment to whatever charges might be brought against them. The scheme of a political settlement in Mexico was preposterous in practice, though tempting to wounded pride. Settlements and colonies were governed, or governed themselves, by laws of material interest, considerations of profit and loss; and no settlers could be imagined less fitted for the requirements of a new colony than a body of embittered politicians, still sore and smarting from a conflict in which they had incurred defeat. Patience, indomitable industry and self-denial were the necessities of every new settlement; and these—even were the colonists of a more suitable class—could scarcely be continued in Mexico, where languor, indolence and ease, are constituent portions of the climate.

Remarked to Mr. Davis that I had always regarded the filibustering expeditions of Lopez against Cuba, and Walker in Nicaragua, as Southern projects for the acquirement of more territory and larger representation in Congress, to balance the increasing free States of the North and West. If his opinions against the feasibility of Southern men colonizing Mexico had been general with his people, how came the Lopez, and more especially the Walker expeditions, to find favor in his section, Walker proposing an American settlement so much nearer the equator? The desire for Cuba could be understood; its enormous slave population, wealth, and command of the Gulf, forming sufficient attractions.

Mr. Davis replied there had been a general desire in the South for Cuba, but none of any consequence for Central America. Neither expedition, however, had been supported by any organized party of his people. The Walker foray in Nicaragua had its main origin in a quarrel between two new New York commercial houses— those of Governor Morgan and Cornelius Vanderbilt, as he understood—for the profits of the Transit Company across the Isthmus. The expedition against Cuba was favored by General Quitman, and had so much of direct Southern sanction as might be drawn from the General's representative position—which was deservedly of the highest— but no more. It was fostered on the statements and promises of Cuban planters anxious for annexation, and promising a liberal coöperation of men and means the moment a landing was effected. These promises went off in smoke, as do all the promises of a tropical and luxurious people for active exertion; and so the matter ended.

In regard to his remarks about settlements in Mexico, it was not his intention—the reverse, in fact—to be understood as suggesting that his people could not, or will not colonize and reclaim the greater part or the whole of that country. His thought merely was, that a settlement of self-exiled politicians and soldiers, acting under the impulse of anger, and with no fixed purposes or habits of industry, and but little capital in money or materials, formed a poor basis for any colonization project of permanent prosperity. His people needed more territory and would continue to need it, their line of expansion running towards Mexico; but this would have to come by natural processes of growth, perhaps assisted, when time was ripe, by some such political and military movements as added Texas to the country. Timely blossom gives timely fruit, and we can no more quicken the healthy growth of a nation by artificial aid than the growth of a child. If restraints be imposed on natural growth, violence may be useful to cast off such restraints, but beyond this can only serve to retard expansion.

Same afternoon, joined Mr. Davis, who was seated with Major-General Miles on the south front of the ramparts, the prisoner seeming to prefer this aspect of the compass.

General Miles remarked that the fortification known as the Rip Raps had already occupied much time, and must have cost the government vast sums of money.

Mr. Davis replied, giving full statistics on the subject up to the period he had ceased to be Secretary of War, adding, that many years ago it had approached completion, but had slowly settled down until the second tier of embrasures reached the sea-level, owing to a spreading of the artificial rock-island on which it has been built. As it was so nearly finished, and might be useful in case of a foreign war, he supposed government would now complete its armament and maintain it as a permanent fort; but if the matter were to do over again, a couple of iron-clads would serve all its purposes better, at less than a tenth of its expense.

General Miles observed, interrogatively, that it was reported John C. Calhoun had made much money by speculations, or favoring the speculations of his friends, connected with this work.

In a moment Mr. Davis started to his feet, betraying much indignation by his excited manner and flushed cheek. It was a transfiguration of friendly emotion, the feeble and wasted invalid and prisoner suddenly forgetting his bonds, forgetting his debility, and ablaze with eloquent anger against this injustice to the memory of one whom he loved and reverenced. Mr. Calhoun, he said, lived a whole atmosphere above any sordid or dishonest thought—was of a nature to which even a mean act was impossible. It was said in every Northern paper that he (Mr. Davis) had carried with him five millions in gold when quitting Richmond—money pilfered from the treasury of the Confederate States—and there was just as much truth in that as in these imputations against Calhoun. One of the worst signs of the times is the looseness with which imputations of dishonesty are made and accepted against public men in eminent station. They who spit against the wind, spit in their own faces, and such charges come back to soil the men who make them. If an individual has any proof of dishonesty against a public man, he should bring his charges in due form, and have an open trial; but when an entire people, or their great majority, greedily accept and believe any unsupported imputation of corruption against a distinguished statesman or other officer, it argues corruption in their own minds, and that they suspect it in others because conscious it would be their own course if endowed with power.

Mr. Davis then entered upon an explanation, too minute for me to follow, of the manner in which these charges against Mr. Calhoun arose from the malice of some speculators, between whose avarice and the public treasury Mr. Calhoun had interposed his pure and powerful influence. Calhoun was a statesman, a philosopher, in the true sense of the grossly abused term—an enthusiast of perfect liberty in representative and governmental action. Wrong, of course, in his conclusions, the opponents of his theory were free to judge him; but Mr. Davis believed the hands of George Washington not more free from the filthiness of bribes, than were those of the departed statesman who had been thus libelled. Every public officer who crosses the schemes of rogues must prepare to pay this penalty. There was not a General in either army of the recent war who was not accused by sutlers and camp-followers of having made fortunes from the exactions which their powers allowed them to impose. While the astronomer dwells in his tower watching the stars, bats may breed and slimy things crawl at will in the foundation-story of his edifice.

August 4th.—Visited Mr. Davis with Captain

Gusson, 3d Pennsylvania Artillery, Officer of the Day. Found prisoner improving. Mentioned that I had spent the previous day on the wreck of the frigate *Congress*, sunk by the *Merrimac*, describing minutely, at his request, the state of the vessel, and the process of elevating sunken vessels by building a bulkhead, etc., and the use of powerful pumps. Mr. Davis appeared much interested, saying the *Congress* had fought gallantly, and that it was in consequence of injuries to the prow of the *Merrimac* from her shot, and not owing to the attack of the *Monitor*, that the *Merrimac* had been compelled to retire. These injuries started a fatal leak, which the weight of armor rendered it impossible to cure; and this was the true cause of the vessel's final failure. Mr. Davis also spoke of the continued advances in engineering skill and mechanical contrivance. When the *Royal George* capsized, she went to the bottom uninjured, and would have been in perfect order had such means for raising sunken vessels been then known. The British Government had made great exertions, and offered large rewards, he believed, to accomplish this result, but without success; and only such small articles, or piecemeal parts, had been regained as the divers could fasten ropes to, and cause to be hauled up. With the exception of the *Merrimac*, no armed vessel of the South had enjoyed a fortunate career, and hers was brief. They were either captured, like the *Atlanta*, while trying to run out to sea, or destroyed by our war vessels and gun-boats while still imperfect and unprepared for the combat. The capture of New Orleans was a great calamity to his cause, but mainly injurious from its sacrifice of the inchoate iron-clads of the Mississippi. With the mouth and headwaters of this vital river in our possession, no energy could have warded off the result beyond a certain time, if the North, with its superior resources of manufacture and preponderance of population, should see fit to persist. Pemberton made a splendid defence of Vicksburg. He had been blamed for remaining there, but this was the last hope of saving the Mississippi and keeping open the beef, and other commissary supplies, of the trans-Mississippi department.

Had General Albert Sidney Johnston lived, Mr. Davis was of opinion, our success down the Mississippi would have been fatally checked at Corinth. This officer best realized his ideal of a perfect commander—large in view, discreet in council, silent as to his own plans, observant and penetrative of the enemy's, sudden and impetuous in action, but of a nerve and balance of judgment which no heat of danger or complexity of manœuvre could upset or bewilder. All that Napoleon said of Dessaix and Kleber, save the slovenly habits of one of them, might be combined and truthfully said of Albert Sidney Johnston. Johnston had been opposed to locating the Confederate Capital at Richmond, alleging that it would involve fighting on the exterior of our circle, in lieu of the centre: and that as the struggle would finally be for whatever point was the capital, it was ill-advised to go so far north, thus shortening the enemy's line of transportation and supply. Whatever value this criticism may have had in a military point of view, added Mr. Davis, there were political necessities connected with Virginia which left no choice in the matter. It was a bold courting of the issue, clearly planting our standard in front of the enemy's line and across his path. Such reflections are of no use now, concluded Mr. Davis, and the Spaniards tell us when a sorrow is asleep not to waken it.

Talking of the financial future of the South, he

believed negro labor requisite for the profitable working of the rice, sugar, and cotton crops. These staples peculiarly demanded the industry of this race. Germans, or Irishmen, could grow tobacco with profit, and for a few years, perhaps, cultivate the other staples; but the climatic influences would overpower their constitutions, and the rice-fields, in particular, prove deadly to any laborers but the black.

To this I opposed my own experience on the Sea Islands of the Southern coast, where I had cognizance of the sanitary condition of an average of fifteen thousand soldiers, black and white, and of all nationalities, for nearly three years; and the result had been that negroes, to the "manor born," had suffered more than any others, white or black, with the exception of the troops from Maine. The work for all had been of the hardest and heaviest; guard-duty night and day along creeks, lagoons and swamps; incessant toil in the trenches and on the works; the severest portion of these labors having been performed on Morris Island, in the month of July. The Southern negro refugees—men, women, and children, living in villages on Port Royal, St. Helena, Edisto, Ladies, and other islands—suffered more from the fevers of the climate than our black troops from the North, and far more than our white troops, who were the healthiest in the whole armies of the Union, with the exception of those from the inland mountains of Maine, and perhaps New Hampshire.

Mr. Davis thought this very possible, but the mortality of the plantation negroes arose from the absence of restraint, and their inability to guide themselves. It was to the master's interest that they should be kept in health by regular hours, wholesome food, and proper periods of rest. The license of sudden freedom proved too much for their ignorant passions, and became perverted into debauchery. It was a feast or a famine with them, and such violent changes of habit never failed to work ruin. While slaves, they were confined to their quarters after certain hours of the night, and thus saved from malarial exposure; while in their new liberty they doubtless remained abroad until whatever hour they pleased. As to the health of the white troops, the excitement of war was in itself a prophylactic. But let the same men try regular labor in time of peace, and a different health-bill would be returned.

CHAPTER XIV.

*Mr. Davis on Negro Character.—The Assassination
of President Lincoln.—How the Prisoner's Food
was Served.—A Solemn and Interesting Statement.*

AUGUST 14TH.—Had been absent in Baltimore on
official business some few days, during which Mr.
Davis sent for me. Called with Captain Evans,
Officer of the Day, and explained my absence. A
pustule, somewhat malignant in character, was
forming on prisoner's face, which was much inflamed and swollen. He reiterated belief that the
casemate was full of malarial poison, caused by the
rising and falling of the tide in the ditch outside
(as previously explained), and wished the Washington people would take quicker means of dis-
patching him, if his death without trial was their
object. That it was so he was led to suspect, for
a trial must develop many things not pleasant to
those in power. In particular it would place the
responsibility for the non-exchange of prisoners
where it belonged.

Called the same evening. Prisoner in a high fever, the swelling of his face spreading to his back and head, with indications of latent erysipelas. Mr. Davis wished he could have with him his faithful servant Robert, who, though a slave, had a moral nobility deserving honor. The negroes had excellent traits of character, but required, for their own sakes, guidance and control. They were docile, as a general rule, easily imbued with religious sentiment, quick in sympathies, and of warm family affection. Their passions, however, were intense and uncontrollable. Slavery had been blamed for their incontinence, but this was unjust. Were the free blacks any less libidinous? The Southern slaves were incomparably more chaste, or less unchaste, than people of the same race in the North. Slavery was a restraint upon promiscuous intercourse, and for commercial reasons, if for none higher. The negroes were improvident to a degree that must reduce them to destitution if not cared for. They had to be provided with fresh seeds for their little garden patches every year, no remonstrances sufficing to make them provide one season for the wants of the next. It was in their affections they were strong, and many of them had excellent traits. His man Robert was the best and most faithful of his race, and had attended him through many serious illnesses. Was with his wife on board the *Clyde*, but might possibly have deserted the sinking ship by this time. Did not think he would, though others with greater claims to keep them faithful were among his enemies.*

August 16*th*.—Called with Captain Gressin, Aide-de-Camp of General Miles, Officer of the Day. Prisoner suffering severely, but in a less critical state, the erysipelas now showing itself in his nose and forehead. Found that a carbuncle was forming on his left thigh, Mr. Davis urging this as proof of a malarial atmosphere in his cell, reiterating his wish that, if the Government wanted to be rid of him without trial, it might take some quicker process.

Prisoner said he had never held much hope for himself since entering Fortress Monroe, and was now losing it for his people. The action and tone in regard to the Richmond elections, gave evidence that the policy of "woe to the conquered" would prevail. What a cruel farce it was to permit an exercise of the elective franchise, with a proviso

* See letter of Mrs. Davis further on, in regard to this worthy servant.

that the electors must cast their ballots for men they despised or hated! Either all pretence of continuing representative government should be abandoned, or free acceptance given to the men indorsed by the people. To ask men who had fought, sacrificed, and lost their all for a cause, to wheel suddenly, and vote into power men they despised as renegades or cowards, was the sin of attempting to seethe the kid in its mother's milk. Better for the South to remain disfranchised forever, than crawl back into office or recognition through such incredible apostasy. Better remain prisoners, than be citizens on such terms. In no district of Virginia could what we called a "loyalist," muster a corporal's guard of men with similar sentiments. Why organize hypocrisy by attempting to force into elective positions men who were not representatives of their alleged constituents—men who could only excite the abhorrence or contempt of ninety-nine in every hundred of the people? Either the South should be declared so many conquered provinces under military rule, or given back the freedom of the ballot. To offer bribes for wholesale falsehood, would be found poor policy; and the men hereafter to create trouble in the South, would not be the gallant and well-born gentlemen who fought loyally, and at every sacrifice of life and property for a cause they believed right, but that small scum of poltroons and renegades who remained "neutral" through the contest, only anxious to avoid danger for themselves, and jump over to the side that won. The former class accepted defeat, and would loyally preserve any obligations that might be imposed on them. The latter were worthless and pitiful intriguers, commanding no popular confidence, chastened by no memories of the struggle; and now that no personal risk could be incurred, would seek to attain popularity—the popularity of demagogues—by re-fanning into flame the passions and prejudices of the ignorant and vulgar. They will be clamorous for Southern rights, now that Southern rights are dead, and out-Herod Herod in their professed devotion to the Southern cause.

August 20*th.*—Called with Captain Evans, Officer of the Day. Mr. Davis suffering great prostration, a cloud of erysipelas covering his whole face and throat. The carbuncle much inflamed. Spirits exceedingly dejected, evinced by anxiety for his wife and children. That he should die without opportunity of rebutting in public trial the imputed stigma of having had share in the conspiracy to assassinate Mr. Lincoln, was referred to frequently and painfully. That history would do him justice, and the criminal absurdity of the charge be its own refutation, he had cheerful confidence while in health; but in his feebleness and despondency, with knowledge how powerful they were who wished to affix this stain, his alarm, lest it might become a reproach to his children, grew an increasing shadow.

Of Mr. Lincoln he then spoke, not in affected terms of regard or admiration, but paying a simple and sincere tribute to his goodness of character, honesty of purpose, and Christian desire to be faithful to his duties according to such light as was given him. Also to his official purity and freedom from avarice. The Southern press labored in the early part of the war to render Mr. Lincoln abhorred and contemptible; but such efforts were against his judgment, and met such opposition as his multiplied cares and labors would permit. Behind Mr. Lincoln, during his first term, stood an infinitely more objectionable and less scrupulous successor (Mr. Hamlin); and the blow that struck down the President of the United States would place that successor in power. When Mr. Lincoln was reinaugurated, the cause of his people was hopeless, or very nearly so—the struggle only justifiable in continuance by its better attitude for obtaining terms; and from no ruler the United States could have, might terms so generous have been expected. Mr. Lincoln was kind of heart, naturally longing for the glory and repose of a second term to be spent in peace. Mr. Johnson, being from the South, dare not offer such liberal treatment; his motives would be impugned. In every embittered national struggle, proposals to assassinate the rival representatives were common, emanating from different classes of men, with different motives: from spies of the enemy, wishing to obtain evidence how such proposals would be received; from fanatics, religious or patriotic, believing the act would prove acceptable to Heaven; from lunatics, driven mad by sufferings connected with the struggle; and from boastful and often cowardly desperadoes, seeking gold and notoriety by attempting, or promising to attempt, the crime. At the time it occurred, Mr. Lincoln's death, even by natural causes, would have been a serious injury to the prospects of the South; but the manner of his taking-off, frenzying the Northern mind, was the last crowning calamity of a despairing and defeated, though righteous cause.

August 21st.—Called with Captain Corlis, on the staff of General Miles, Officer of the Day. Prostration increased, and the erysipelas spreading. Deemed it my duty to send a communication to Major-General Miles, reporting that I found the State-prisoner, Davis, suffering severely from erysipelas in the face and head, accompanied by the usual prostration attending that disease. Also that he had a small carbuncle on his left thigh, his condition denoting a low state of the vital forces.

August 23d.—Called with Captain Evans, 3d Pennsylvania Artillery, Officer of the Day. Prisoner a little improved, febrile symptoms subsiding. Had no appetite for ordinary food, but found the coolness and moisture of fruits agreeable. Said he had concluded not to lose any more spoons for me, but would retain the one that morning sent with his breakfast. Unless things took a change, he would not require it long.

[This was an allusion to the desire some of the guards had to secure trophies of anything Mr. Davis had touched. They had carried away his brier-wood pipe, and from time to time taken five of the spoons sent over with his meals from my quarters. The meals were sent over by a bright little mulatto boy named Joe, who handed them to the sergeant of the guard outside the casemate, who passed them through the window to the lieutenant of the guard in the outer cell, by whom they were handed to the prisoner through the grated doors of the inside room, the keys of which were held by the Officer of the Day. No knife and fork being allowed the prisoner, "lest he should commit suicide," his food had to be cut up before being sent over—a needless precaution, it always seemed to me, and more likely to produce than prevent the act, by continually keeping the idea that it was expected before the prisoner's mind. It was in returning the trays from Mr. Davis to my quarters that the spoons were taken— an annoyance obviated by his retaining one for use. This only changed the form of trophy, however; napkins that he had used being the next class of prizes seized and sent home to sweethearts by loyal warders at the gates.]

Mr. Davis expressed some anxiety as to his present illness. He was not one of those who, when in trouble, wished to die. Great invalids seldom had this wish, save when protracted sufferings had weakened the brain. Suicides were commonly of the robuster class—men who had never been brought close to death nor thought much about it seriously. A good old Bishop once remarked, that "dying was the last thing a man should think about," and the mixture of wisdom and quaint humor in the phrase had impressed Mr. Davis. Even to Christians, with the hope of an immortal future for the soul, the idea of physical annihilation—of parting forever from the tenement of flesh in which we have had so many joys and sorrows—was one full of awe, if not terror. What it must be to the unbeliever, who entertained absolute and total annihilation as his prospect, he could not conceive. Never again to hear of wife or children—to take the great leap into black vacuity, with no hope of meeting in a brighter and happier life the loved ones left behind, the loved ones gone before!

He had more reasons than other men, and now more than ever, to wish for some prolongation of life, as also to welcome death. His intolerable sufferings and wretched state argued for the grave as a place of rest. His duties to the cause he had represented, and his family, made him long to be continued on the footstool, in whatever pain or misery, at least until by the ordeal of a trial he could convince the world he was not the monster his enemies would make him appear, and that no wilful departures from the humanities of war had stained the escutcheon of his people. Errors, like all other men, he had committed; but stretched now on a bed from which he might never rise, and looking with the eyes of faith, which no walls could bar, up to the throne of Divine mercy, it was his comfort that no such crimes as men laid to his charge reproached him in the whispers of his conscience.

"They charge me with crime, Doctor, but God knows my innocence. I indorsed no measure that was not justified by the laws of war. Failure is all forms of guilt in one to men who occupied my position. Should I die, repeat this for the sake of my people, my dear wife, and poor darling children. Tell the world I only loved America, and that in following my State I was only carrying out doctrines received from reverenced lips in my early youth, and adopted by my judgment as the convictions of riper years."

Mr. Davis spoke with intense earnestness—the solemnity of a dying man, though not then, in my judgment, in any immediate danger. His words, as quoted, were taken down on my return to quarters, and are here given for what each reader may think them worth. They certainly impressed me as sincere, and as if—whether true or not, judged by the standard of law—the speaker uttered them in the good faith of a religious man, who thought death might very possibly be near, if not imminent and certain.

CHAPTER XV.

Southern Non-Belligerents.—The Ant-Lion and its Habits.—Mr. Davis on the Future of the Southern Blacks.

AUGUST 24TH.—Visited Mr. Davis with Captain Titlow, Officer of the Day. Found him slightly better in body and mind. Expressed hope that no sensational reports of his illness had appeared in the newspapers to alarm his wife more than necessary. His hope was faint, however. The swarm of newspaper correspondents, more than quadrupled by the war, no longer finding food for their pens in camps or on battle-fields, had to seize every item of the slightest interest and swell it into importance by exaggeration, in order to retain their employment. Spoke of the superior literary and inventive powers of our correspondents during the war. To contrast the dry official report of some affair of outposts or the skirmish line, in which half a dozen men on either side had been killed or wounded, with the wonderfully enlarged and intensely colored mirage of the same appearing some few days subsequently in the Northern press, formed an amusing and amazing study, giving one a higher ideal of man's imaginative power. The Southern press, on the contrary, was short of printers, short of paper, and all other requisites for exciting journalism, insomuch that latterly only the meagerest skeletons of events could appear; and even official documents, and debates of the highest consequence, had to be briefly epitomized.

Mr. Davis said the press of the South had enjoyed more liberty and given more trouble to its government than that of the North. Properly conducted, its power was an important adjunct to the machinery of war; but engineering it was a complex study, calling for special education in its professor. The only men still remaining vindictively belligerent and anxious to perpetuate trouble in the South—so far as he knew, and as their words could reach—would be found in the small-fry of little country editors, and certain classes of civilians who had been exempted from military service by special legislation, the purchase of substitutes, or the procurement of details. It was the non-belligerents of actual conflict who had always been and would remain most ferociously belligerent in speech and writing. Not having borne arms in the struggle, they might claim rewards for their loyalty or neutrality in Federal patronage, or offices to be filled by popular vote; and such claims would likely be allowed by our people to the exclusion of those fearless and honorable men, who—having fought, failed, and accepted defeat—were now only anxious to erase all painful souvenirs and legacies of the unfortunate and unavailing strife.

Observing me brush away with my foot some crumbs scattered near his bedside, Mr. Davis asked me to desist; they were for a mouse he was domesticating—the only living thing he had now power to benefit. The drawback to this companionship was, that the crumbs called forth a swarm of red ants as well as the mouse; and he suggested, with a smile, that a few ant-lions should be caught and brought in from the beach. Placed in a cigar-box, with some fine sand and a lump of sugar, or a few dead locusts, to attract the ants, they would soon rid him of his insect visitors, and afford him, though on a small scale, the nearest approach to sport he could now have.

Finding my curiosity excited, Mr. Davis then described the ant-lion with much minuteness and

pleasant humor, saying it was next to the bee as an
interesting study in natural history. It is about
the size of a small, elongated pea, three legs on
each side, a forceps proportionably immense arm-
ing its head, and between these nippers a sharp
stiletto, which can be drawn in or thrown out at
pleasure. It is found all along the Southern coast,
and would seem to have a difficult problem in
supporting life. It is painfully slow of movement,
always walking backward and dragging its heavy
forceps along the ground behind it; while the
ants, on which it chiefly preys, are extremely
active. Nature, however, has compensated by
subtlety what the ant-lion lacks in spring. It
digs a funnel-shaped hole in the fine sand of the
Southern coast, circular at the top, of an inch
diameter and an inch in depth. At the bottom it
secretes itself in the sand, only its forceps pro-
truding. These pitfalls are located about an inch
or so from the stems of shrubs or tufts of grass—
the ants flocking to these latter, because finding
in them a species of grass-louse called the ant-cow,
which the ant milks by suction as its favorite
food, the cows not resisting lest worse befall them,
and not appearing injured by the process. While
the ants are thus hastening to their food, some one

of them will approach the brink of the ant-lion's pitfall, and instantly the fine sand of the edge gives way, precipitating the unwary traveller to the bottom. Here he is seized by the forceps, and firmly held, while the stiletto is driven through his body. His juices are soon sucked dry by the secreted monster of the cave, and then with one jerk of the forceps, the carcass is flung up and out two or three inches beyond the edge of the funnel —a distance as much as if a man were thrown one hundred and fifty times his length. Should the ant, when first tumbling, escape the grasp of the forceps, and seek to clamber out of the trap, the ant-lion foils the attempt by jerking little jets of sand on the body and across the path of his flying victim, who is soon stunned, bewildered, and losing his foot-grasp on the slippery sides, falls back a helpless prey to his destroyer. Mr. Davis, when on the coast of Georgia, many years ago, had often spent hours in watching them, and their whole performance could be witnessed by placing one in a cigar-box half filled with fine sand, and dropping in some sugar or a dead locust to attract the ants. The ant-lion would not be in the box half a day, before commencing to earn his livelihood by digging out his trap. So great was the habit of subtlety in this insect, that when moving from place to place, it always burrowed along just a little beneath the surface of the sand; and he had heard, if compelled to cross a stone, log, or other obstruction, that it seized a chip or leaf with its forceps, thereby covering its body, as it slowly and painfully toiled backward. This, however, he could not verify from personal observation.

Every conversation of this kind with Mr. Davis recalled the saying of some eminent writer whose name has escaped me, that "it is a noble thing to know how to take a country walk," or words containing that idea, but more concisely and vividly expressed. Educated by the microscope and habits of observation, we become afraid of treading on some of God's beautiful little things at every step.

August 25th.—Called upon Mr. Davis, accompanied by Captain Gresson of the staff of Major-General Miles, Officer of the Day. The Captain gave me an order from General Miles, allowing State-prisoner Davis to have a knife and fork with his meals hereafter. Mr. Davis was pleased, but said he had learned many new uses to which a spoon could be put when no other implement was accessible. In particular, it was the best peach-peeler ever invented, and he illustrated as he spoke on a fruit that lay on his table. Denying him a knife and fork lest he should commit suicide, he said, was designed to represent him to the world as an atrocious criminal, so harrowed by remorse that the oblivion of death would be welcome. His early shackles had partly the same object, but still more to degrade his cause.

Prisoner's health very delicate, but the erysipelas subsiding. Asked could he soon resume his walks in the open air? The change of scene being a great delight, and the exercise improving his sleep.

He referred to an account he had been reading of an attack on a negro named Davenport, in Connecticut, for marrying or living with a white woman. Also, to the New York riots, in which mobs rose suddenly upon the blacks, hanging them to lamp-posts and roasting them at slow fires. The papers bore evidence, from all sections, of increasing hostility between the races, and this was but part of the penalty the poor negro had to pay for freedom. The more political equality was given or approached, the greater must become the social antagonism of the races. In the South, under slavery, there was no such feeling, because

there could be no rivalry. Children of the white
master were often suckled by negroes, and sported
during infancy with black playmates. Old enough
to engage in manlier exercise, it was under black
huntsmen the young whites took their first lessons
in field-sports. They fished, shot, and hunted
together, eating the same bread, drinking from the
same cup, sleeping under the same tree with their
negro guide. In public conveyances there was no
social exclusion of the blacks, nor any dislike
engendered by competition between white and
negro labor. In the bed-chamber of the planter's
daughter it was common for a negro girl to sleep,
as half attendant half companion; and while there
might be, as in all countries and amongst all races,
individual instances of cruel treatment, he was
well satisfied that between no master and laboring
classes on earth had so kindly and regardful a
feeling subsisted. To suppose otherwise required
a violation of the known laws of human nature.
Early associations of service, affection and support
were powerful. To these self-interest joined. The
horse we hire for a day may be fed or not fed,
groomed or not groomed, when returned to the
livery-stable. The horse owned by us, and for
which we have paid a thousand or fifteen hundred

dollars, is an object both of pride and solicitude. His grooming, stabling, and feeding are cared for. If sick he is doctored, and cured if possible. When at work, it is the owner's interest that he shall not be overtaxed.

The attainment of political equality by the negro will revolutionize all this. It will be as if our horses were given the right of intruding into our parlors; or brought directly into competition with human labor, no longer aiding it but as rivals. Put large gangs of white laborers, belonging to different nationalities, at work beside each other, and feuds will probably break out. Endeavor to supplant a thousand Irishmen working on a levee or canal by a thousand Germans ready to accept lower wages, or *vice versa*, and military power will be required to keep the peace. Emancipation does this upon a gigantic scale and in the most aggravated form. It throws the whole black race into direct and aggressive competition with the laboring classes of the whites; and their ignorance of the blacks, presuming on their freedom, will embitter every difference. The principle of compensation prevails everywhere through nature, and the negroes will have to pay, in harsher social restrictions and treatment, for the attempt to invest them with political equality. To endow them with the ballot by Act of Congress was impossible, until the trunk of the Constitution, already stripped of many branches once full of shade and pleasant singing-birds, was torn up by the roots. Each State had the privilege of deciding the qualifications of its own citizens; and some of the States most clamorous for universal negro suffrage in the South, where such a measure would send unlettered blacks to both Houses of Congress, and pass the State Legislature and judiciary altogether into their hands, themselves refused the ballot to the negro, though not numerous enough in any district to decide the majority of a pound-keeper.

Took issue with Mr. Davis on the labor question. What necessity for competition in a country so vast, and only partially developed, as the South? The relations of the races would adjust themselves, under the laws of supply and demand, and the whites still owned their old plantations and other property, which was their capital; and to this the labor of the blacks would have to bow. White labor could not long remain, nor to any great extent, in competition with black. It had accumulative energies, guided by intelligence, which must soon lift it into the employing class; while the blacks, if so incapable of thrift as he seemed to think, must remain hewers of wood and drawers of water for ever. The antagonisms of so violent a revolution in the labor-system of the South were natural, but must soon fade out. There never had been any desire North to give the negroes social equality; but our pride, not less than sense of justice, demanded that there should be no political bar to their improving their own condition to equal that of the whites, if they possessed the capacity for such elevation. As to the outrages upon the blacks in New York, they were the work of a few abandoned and maddened wretches—men certainly not representing nor belonging to the party in control of our national destinies. It was a riot to resist the draft, and the inoffensive blacks became objects of vengeance, from the democratic cry that the war making the draft necessary was a "war for the nigger." The case in Connecticut was a protest in violent and illegal form of certain turbulent whites against the intermarrying of the races. It was lawless, of course, and one of the rioters had lost his life at the hands of the black, who was held justifiable. Nevertheless, the sentiment that prompted the attack—one of the opposition to such deteriorating interminglements—was all but universal, and offered sufficient guarantee that the dominant race would never suffer material injury to its blood or character from the political equality of the negroes.

Mr. Davis said no argument could make us agree, for we occupied different planes of observation. There could be no problem of the negro at the North, for they were too few to be of consequence; and each census showed their number diminishing. It was in the Cotton States, where they equalled, and in many districts largely outnumbered the whites, that the adjustment of relationship would prove impossible under such ideas as now threatened to prevail in the Federal Government. As for himself and his people, they were now only passengers in the Ship of State—no longer of the crew, nor with places on the quarterdeck; and must take, he supposed, whatever decision of the question the powers that had lifted themselves above the Constitution might see fit to impose.

CHAPTER XVI.

Mr. Davis on Fenianism.—Highly Important.—
His Views of Reconstruction.

AUGUST 26TH.—Called upon Mr. Davis, accompanied by Captain Evans, 3d Pennsylvania Artillery, Officer of the Day. Health slightly improved, and spirits decidedly more cheerful.

Mr. Davis said his imprisonment had one advantage, giving him time to re-read Bancroft's History of the United States, and read Macaulay's History of England—the latter something he had long wished, but could not find time for. The system of settlement and confiscations under Cromwell, in Ireland, was precisely what his people were now threatened with. The cry then was, "To * * * * or Connaught!" whither an attempt was made to drive and herd together the whole people. Whole estates, and even counties, were confiscated by orders in council, on no other plea than that the proprietors were either of the Irish race, or, being born on Irish soil, had Irish sympathies or habits. This history now threat-

ened to repeat itself in the United States, the cry
only varying to read, "To * * * * or Mexico!"
and the locality changed from Ireland to the
South. There was no excuse for it here; there
had been some in Ireland. Between the conquering forces of Cromwell and the Irish there were
essential differences of race, religion, habits, laws,
and hopes. There had been war for centuries, and
no promise of future tranquillity on less rigorous
terms. Were the races the same, though controlled by different ideas; their religion, habits,
and laws almost identical, and with only a single
internecine war to interrupt the harmony of their
joint occupation of the continent—there was the
further parallel that both countries suffered for
loyalty to what each regarded as the rightful
government; Ireland, for devotion to the Royal
Family of the Stuarts; and the South, for its
fidelity to the principles defined by the Constitution
of 1787.

The present Fenian movement for Ireland was a
farce to make angels weep. The last attempt was
in 1848, when the population of Ireland was more
than a million larger—the movement originating
at home, and all Europe in a convulsive and vol-
canic condition. History gave no example of an

oppressed race that had accepted exile, returning with success to liberate their native land. The aristocratic refugees of the French Revolution, indeed, got back to their country, but only under the swords of a combination in which England, Austria, Russia, Prussia, and the German States were enlisted, with their whole military resources. It was a mere catch-penny clamor of designing demagogues in its cis-Atlantic aspect; nor could he see that in Ireland there was organization, or even a vigorous purpose to accomplish the object proposed. England's control of the sea was absolute, at least so near home against any less combination than the navies of France and America. To land men or arms in any sufficient quantity in Ireland, would require some desperate sea-fights by navy with navy, and a transport fleet, costing for vessels and their equipment not less than some hundred millions. The men engaged in this matter must be either fools or rogues. He had no special cause to love England, nor dislike, but such impracticable and pigmy threatenings of her empire would be ludicrous if not too sad. Against the rocks of her coast, storm-clouds of a thousandfold the Fenian power had dashed with clamor of waves and mist of spray, but next morning the sun shone bright again, the air was calm, and only in a shore strewn with wrecks could evidence be found of any past commotion.

Asking Mr. Davis what his views in regard to the reconstruction of the Union, he spoke pretty nearly verbatim as follows; this report not being condensed as with other conversations, but taken down in full from memory, immediately on my return to quarters:

"We could not otherwise define reconstruction, than as a renewal to and by all the States, of all the rights, privileges, duties, immunities, and obligations prescribed and recognized by the Constitution, or original compact of Union. There were several possible alternatives to this plan of reconstruction:

"1st. Consolidation: the swallowing up of all State governments by the General Government, making the whole country one State, only divided into provinces for easier administration, but connected as one entity of policy and power.

"2d. Territorialism: the control of the Southern States by a Congress and Executive representing only the Northern States—that is, colonial vassalage and government by authority of greater force.

"3d. By open supervision and usurpation to establish a despotism over North and South, while yet preserving a certain Republican form.

"In replying to one who served through the war for no other purpose, as you avow, than to defend and maintain the Union as defined by the Constitution," continued Mr. Davis, "there can be no necessity for considering any other policy than that of re-establishing the relations of all the States and their citizens to each other and the United States Government.

"Every man's experience must teach him that quarrels between friends are best healed when they are healed most promptly. The alienation which was at first a pain, becomes by time habitual, and the mantle of charity being withdrawn, the faults of each become more and more distinct to the other, and thus the bitterest hates naturally spring from the ashes of the closest friendship.

"It is therefore probably to be regretted that so much delay has occurred in the work of reconstruction, because of the enhancement thereby of the difficulties in the way of speedy and cordial reconciliation. This opinion is qualified as 'probable,' because of my want of recent intercourse with the people. A short time before the close of the war, the idea was infused into my people, as you are well aware, that if they would cease resistance, the Union would be restored, and all their rights of person and property respected, save the property held in slaves, which would be a question for the courts. I have no doubt that a majority— a very large majority—of the Southern people accepted this proposed settlement with singleness of purpose; and would, if confidingly and generously treated, have been now industriously engaged in repairing their wrecked fortunes, without any thought of again resisting or obstructing the General Government in its ordinary functions.

"How far the public wealth would by this course have been increased, the public expenditures lessened, may be measured by many hundred millions of dollars. If it be true that much has been lost, morally and materially, by delay, it would seem that true policy indicates the promptest action in what is termed Reconstruction. The North says we have done evil, and when bidding us 'cease to do evil' should not prevent us 'learning to do well.' This can only be done by removing all impediments to the exercise of State functions and the re-enjoyment of such civil and political rights as are left us in the Union.

"Each House of Congress is judge of the election and qualification of its own members. The Constitution has settled the question of representation. A constituency may lose its rights for a time by selecting ineligible persons to be its representatives; but the right of representation is not impaired thereby, and the mistake or abuse may be remedied by a new election. Test-oaths are evil continually and only evil. They restrain those honorable men who require no fetters, while men of a different class will either take them perjuriously or with a 'mental reservation.' All history has proved them ineffectual and something worse.

"Our forefathers emigrated to a wilderness, and waged the war of the Revolution, to have and to hold a government founded on the consent of the governed. They consulted and compromised with each other to establish a voluntary Union. If that idea is to be followed, confidence, generosity, fraternity, and not test-oaths, disabilities, and armies quartered in the interior, must be relied upon to restore the Union and make it re-effective for the ends for which it was formed.

"Reconstruction," continued Mr. Davis, "cannot properly involve or be made to depend on those social problems which have arisen from the sudden disruption of the relations existing between the white and the black races in the Southern States. These problems belong to the several States, and must have treatment according to the different circumstances of each. No general rule can properly be made applicable to all, and it will prove unfortunate if the subject is controlled by distant and but poorly-informed, if not prejudiced authority. The self-interest of individuals and communities, together with the demand for labor so far exceeding the supply, may safely be left to protect the laborer.

"The public actions of the Southern State Conventions furnishes conclusive evidence of the desire of the Southern people to resume their position in the Union; and it must strike all observers with surprise, that while those who strove so desperately to leave the Union, are now so earnestly endeavoring to reassume their places in it, it is the very men who sent fire and sword to destroy them, or compel them to return, who now bar the door and deny them readmission to that very condition to which it was throughout the war proclaimed to be their first and last duty to return. Solitary reflection," concluded Mr. Davis, "has given me no key to the mysterious origin of this change in

Northern opinion, which I find evidenced in every newspaper that reaches me; and perhaps my own sad state has tinged with its gloom the vista of the future, if, thus alienated, disjointed, and adrift, the country should be visited with such trials of foreign war, either with France or England, or both, as are now so often suggested in the public journals of America, and their extracts from the European press."

This conversation impressed me much, and has been recorded with peculiar care, Mr. Davis delivering it with great deliberation and earnestness, as though the subject were one upon which he had been reflecting. It is as nearly as possible reproduced in his own words, without abridgment, and may, perhaps, be of some suggestive value—perhaps of none. Let the wise of the land determine.

CHAPTER XVII.

*Mr. Davis Seriously Ill.—Change of Quarters Offi-
cially Recommended.—The Pictures and Poetry
of the Bible.—Lafayette's Imprisonment.—Marvellous Memory and Great Variety of Knowledge.
—Mr. Davis on Female Lecturers.—The True
Mission of Women.*

SEPTEMBER 1ST.—Was called at daylight by Captain Titlow, Officer of the Day, to see State-prisoner
Davis, who appeared rapidly sinking, and was believed in a critical condition. The carbuncle on
his thigh was much inflamed, his pulse indicating
extreme prostration of the vital forces. The
erysipelas which had subsided now reappeared, and
the febrile excitement ran very high. Prescribed
such remedies, constitutional and topical, as were
indicated; but always had much trouble to per-
suade him to use the stimulants so urgently needed
by his condition. Let me here say, however, that
in docility and a strict adherence to whatever
regimen was prescribed Mr. Davis was the model
patient of my practice. He seemed to regard the

224

doctor as captain of the patient's health, and obeyed every direction, however irksome, disagreeable, or painful, with military exactness.

Mr. Davis renewed his complaints of the vitiated atmosphere of the casemate, declaring it to be noxious and pestilential from the causes before noticed. Mould gathered upon his shoes, showing the dampness of the place; and no animal life could prosper in an atmosphere that generated these hyphomycetous fungi. From the rising and falling of the tides in the loose foundations of the casemate, mephitic fungi emanated, the spores of which, floating in the air, were thrown off in such quantities, and with such incessant repetitions of reproduction, as to thoroughly pervade the atmosphere, entering the lungs and blood with every breath, and redeveloping their poisonous qualities in the citadel of life. Peculiar classes of these fungi were characteristics of the atmosphere in which cholera and other forms of plague were most rankly generated, as had been established by the Rev. Mr. Osborne, in a long and interesting series of experimental researches with the achromatic microscope during the cholera visitation of 1854 in England. Men in robust health might defy these miasmatic influences; but to him, so physically reduced, the atmosphere that generated mould found no vital force sufficient to resist its poisonous inhalation.

Assured Mr. Davis that his opinion on the matter had for some time been my own, and that on several occasions I had called the attention of Major-General Miles to the subject. Satisfied that the danger was now serious if he were longer continued in such an atmosphere, I would make an official report on the subject to the General Commanding, recommending a change of quarters.

Referring to the consolation he derived from the Bible, Mr. Davis spoke of its power to present beautiful and comforting pictures, full of promise and instruction, apposite to every situation of joy or calamity in life, but never so well appreciated as in our moments of deepest despondency and sorrow. No picture had impressed him more than that of Abraham preparing to sacrifice Isaac, his son—the son of promise. The grim fidelity of the narrative only heightened its irresistible pathos. The sad journey to Mount Moriah of Abraham with his two young men and Isaac, the father only knowing the terrible burden of the duty imposed on him by angelic order. The halt when they came in sight of the hill of sacrifice. Abraham's brief, sad order to his two attendants: "Abide ye here with the ass, and I and the lad will go up yonder and worship." The silent procession to the place of sacrifice, Isaac with the wood upon his shoulders, the father striding along in dumb despair, with the knife in one hand and the torch in the other. Isaac's child-like inquiry, "Behold the fire and the wood, but where is the lamb for a burnt-offering?" and Abraham's reply of faith, Jehovah jireh—"My son, God will provide it." Last scene of all, the son of promise bound on the faggots his young shoulders had so joyously borne; the miserable father bending over the lad he loved, the joy of his old age, grasping the knife that was to slay him. Then comes the Divine interference, in the voice of the angel once again. The promise of faith, Jehovah jireh, is redeemed, and behind the father, as he turns, beholds a ram entangled in a thicket by his horns. In many an hour of bitter calamity the words Jehovah jireh had been his only consolation. When troubles that seemed hopeless of extrication encompassed him on every side, the words Jehovah jireh were full of whispering consolation to his spirit. His mind had framed the picture in gold, and it was but one of a thousand.

Another beautiful picture Mr. Davis spoke of

as suspended in the gallery through which his thoughts, in their despondent moments, loved to trace. Dark night over Jerusalem. A little group, a Master and faithful followers, emerging from the gates. As they descend into the valley, their mantles are drawn more closely round their hurrying and silent figures, for the night-wind is chill and damp. Where the little brook Kedron runs, we see them picking their way across the stones; and now they move silently up the Mount of Olives into the Garden of Gethsemane. That night, before quitting Jerusalem, they had sat at supper—a Supper since commemorated in all Christian lands; and as they sat and did eat, the Master foretold that one of these followers should betray Him. And now they had arrived at the garden; and the Master, calling three of His most beloved disciples, leads them apart from the others, and breathes into their ears as they move along in the double shadows of night and the olive grove, that "His soul is sorrowful even unto death." When sufficiently removed from the larger group, as they approached a darker cluster of olives, the Master says to the three, "Tarry ye here and watch." In the great agony that is upon Him, He longs to be alone. Already the burden of the sins of mankind, whom He so loves that He is about to die for them, grows too weighty for his tenement of flesh. About a stone's cast from the lesser group, the Master falls upon the ground, and prays with thick sobs into the pitying darkness, that if it be possible, this Hour may pass from Him—the human in His nature crying out under its intolerable burden, "Take away this cup from me; for with thee, O Father, all things are possible." But again the Divine will becomes paramount; faith reasserts her ascendancy; and bowing His head upon His hands, the Master sobs, "Nevertheless, not my will, but thine be done." And here, as with Abraham on the hill of Jehovah jireh, an angel appears to strengthen and comfort the obedient heart. Mr. Davis said he could bear to witness the agonizing scene of the garden, but wished to blot from his memory the unfaithfulness of the watchers.

Mr. Davis again spoke of the wretchedness of being constantly watched—of feeling that a human eye, inquisitive and pitiless, was fixed upon all his movements night and day. This was one of the torments imposed on the Marquis de Lafayette in the dungeons of Magdeburgh and Olmutz. Indeed, the parallel between their prison lives, if not in some other respects, was remarkable. Lafayette was denied the use of a knife or fork, lest he should commit self-destruction. He was confined in a casemate, or dungeon, of the two most powerful fortresses of Prussia first, and then Austria. While in Magdeburgh, he found a friend in the humane physician, who repeatedly reported that the prisoner could not live unless allowed to breathe purer air than that of his cell; and on this recommendation—the Governor at first answering that he "was not ill enough yet"—the illustrious prisoner was at length allowed to take the air—sometimes on foot, at other times in a carriage, but always accompanied by an officer with drawn sword and two armed guards.

Mr. Davis then narrated, with great spirit and minuteness, the efforts made by Count Lally-Tolendal, assisted by Dr. Eric Bollmann, of Hanover, and Mr. Huger, of South Carolina, to effect Lafayette's liberation. Mr. Huger was a young gentleman of Huguenot extraction; and Lafayette, upon landing near Georgetown, South Carolina, accompanied by Baron De Kalb, had first been a guest of Major Huger, the father of his rescuer. Dr. Bollmann's visit to Vienna, where he remained six months, lulling suspicion by pretending to study or practise medicine; his there meeting with young Huger, and the manner in which these two cautious, though daring, men mutually discovered to each other their similarity of object; the code of signals which they gradually established with the prisoner, and his final rescue for some brief hours from captivity by their exertions, together with his re-arrest and the capture and terrible punishment inflicted on his rescuers—all these points Mr. Davis recited with a vividness which made each feature in the successive scenes pass before the mental eye as though in the unrolling of a panorama. Huger and Bollmann were heavily ironed around the neck, and chained to the floors of separate dungeons, in utter darkness. Once every half hour the Austrian Officer of the Day entered, flashed a dark lantern into their faces to identify them and see that they still lived, and then carefully examined every link of the chains binding their necks to the floor and shackling their feet and wrists. This treatment lasted, night and day, for six months, the prisoners being almost skeletons when finally obtaining their release, which was secured by the representations of General Washington, the powerful advocacy of Mr. Fox, and the Liberals in the British Parliament,

and the humane sympathy of the Count Metrou-
skie, who wielded a powerful influence in the
Austrian court. Lafayette, however, even in his
second imprisonment, was never shackled; and
though treated with the utmost cruelty, no indignities were offered to his person, save that he
was robbed of his watch and some other trinkets
on being recommitted, reduced to a single suit of
clothes, and stripped of every little comfort that
had been previously allowed him, save such occasional betterments of food—his regulation diet
being bread and water—as were certified by his
medical attendant to be necessary for the support
of life.

It may be here remarked, that the power of
memory possessed by Mr. Davis appeared almost
miraculous—a single perusal of any passage that
interested either his assent or denial enabling him
to repeat it almost verbatim, when eulogizing its
logic or combating what he considered its errors.
This wonderful gift of memorizing, and apparent
universality of knowledge, were remarked by every
Officer of the Day as well as myself, Mr. Davis
having kindly relations with all, and conversation
suited to each visitor. As instances of this—at
which I was not present myself, but heard related

from the officers immediately after their occurrence—let me mention two conversations.

An Officer of the Day, very fond of dogs, and believing himself well posted in all varieties of that animal, once entered the prisoner's cell, followed by a bull-terrier or some other breed of belligerent canine. Mr. Davis at once commenced examining and criticising the dog's points with all the minuteness of a master, thence gliding into a general review of the whole race of pointers, setters, and retrievers; terriers, bull-dogs, German poodles, greyhounds, blood-hounds, and so forth; the result of his conversation being best given in the words of the dog-fancying officer: "Well, I thought I knew something about dogs, but hang me if I won't get appointed Officer of the Day as often as I can, and go to school with Jeff. Davis." On another occasion "some lewd fellows of the baser sort" in the garrison had been fighting a main of cocks; the Lieutenant of the Guard in the outer room being the proud possessor of the victorious chanticleer. It thus came to pass that the conquering bird, with dripping plumage, was brought under the prisoner's notice, and again the same scene as with the dog-fancier was repeated in regard to game-cocks and fighting-birds of all varieties—Mr. Davis describing the popularity of the sport in Mexico, and adding, that when a boy in Mississippi, he had seen only too much of it, until found out and forbidden by his parents.

On quitting Mr. Davis this day, and in compliance with the order of Major-General Miles, I transmitted to headquarters the following report:

Office of the Chief Medical Officer,
FORT MONROE, VA., September 1, 1865.

BREVET MAJOR-GENERAL N. A. MILES,
Commanding Military District,
Fort Monroe, Va.

GENERAL:—I have the honor to report prisoner Davis still suffering from the effects of a carbuncle. The erysipelas of the face had entirely subsided, but yesterday reappeared. His health is evidently rapidly declining.

I remain, General, very respectfully,

Your obedient servant,

JOHN J. CRAVEN,

Bv't Lieut.-Col. U. S. Vol's, and C. M. O.,
Military District, Fort Monroe, Va.

September 2d.—Visited prisoner early, accompanied by Captain Sanderson, 3d Pennsylvania Artillery, Officer of the Day. Condition of Mr.

Davis may be seen in the two following reports, the first being the ordinary one addressed to Major-General Miles, accompanied by a verbal recommendation (often previously made), for a change of quarters. The second, a fuller report, covering the same point, in official form, intended to be transmitted by General Miles to the authorities at Washington. The routine report merely ran:

"I have the honor to report prisoner Davis's condition not perceivably different from that of yesterday: very feeble; no appetite."

The second report, of same date, intended for transmission to the War Department, ran as follows:

Office of the Chief Medical Officer,
FORT MONROE, VA., September 2, 1865.

BREVET MAJOR-GENERAL N. A. MILES,
Commanding Military District,
Fort Monroe, Va.

GENERAL:—I have the honor to report that I was called to see prisoner Davis on the 24th day of May last. I found him very feeble; prematurely old; all the evidence of an iron will, but extremely reduced in physical structure. As he continued to fail, changes were suggested in his prison life, and kindly granted; his food was changed from prison food to a liberal diet; the guards and light were removed from his room; he was permitted to walk in the open air, and to have miscellaneous reading. Indeed, everything was done for him to render him comfortable as a prisoner.

Within the last week, I have noticed a great change in the prisoner. He has become despondent and dull, a very unnatural condition for him. He is evidently breaking down. Save a small patch of erysipelas upon his face, and a carbuncle upon one of his limbs, no pointed disease, but general prostration.

I am of opinion that it may be in a measure attributed to the dampness of his room, for I have noticed lately a great change in the atmosphere of the casemates, and would respectfully recommend that he be removed from the room he now occupies to some other apartment. I have no other suggestions to make as to his treatment. He has the best of food and stimulants.

I remain, General, very respectfully,

Your obedient servant,

(Signed)   JOHN J. CRAVEN,

Bv't Lieut.-Col. and Surg. U. S. Vol's and C. M. O.,

Military District, Fort Monroe, Va.

On this occasion, Mr. Davis referred to some remark of Miss Anna Dickenson, hostile to himself, which he had seen in the papers; also recalling that he had heard of the lady's honoring Fort Monroe with her presence some six weeks before— he supposed to derive her inspiration from an actual view of his casemate, or possibly to catch a secret view of him through the admiring favor of General Miles or some smitten officer. He had noticed that Miss Dickenson had figured largely upon the lecturing stage, and had undeniable talent, but the talent rather of a Mænad or Pythoness than most of the mild virgins who worshipped Vesta and kept the fires of faith and charity forever burning on her pure altars. Woman's appearance in the political arena was a deplorable departure from the golden path which nature had marked out for her. The male animal was endowed with more than sufficient belligerency for all purposes of healthy agitation; and woman's part in the social economy, as she had been made beautiful and gentle, should be to soothe asperities, rather than deepen and make more rough the cross-tracks plowed in the road of life by the diverging passions and opinions of men. It was a revolutionary age; transpositions and novelty

were the fancies of the day, and woman on the
political rostrum was only an outcropping of the
disorganized and disorganizing ideas now in control
of the popular mind. The clamor of certain classes
of women for admission to the professions and employments heretofore engrossed by men, was
another phase of the same malady. They demanded to be made self-supporting, forgetful that
their most tender charm and safest armor lay in
helplessness. Woman's office embraced all the
sweetest and holiest duties of suffering humanity.
Her true altar is the happy fireside, not the forum
with its foul breath and distracting clamors.
Physically unable to defend themselves from
injury or insult, their weakness is a claim which
the man must be utterly base who disregards.
The highest test of civilization is the deference
paid to women. They are like the beautiful vines
of the South, winding around the rugged forest-
trees and clothing them with beauty; but let them
attempt living apart from this support and they
will soon trail along the ground in muddy and
trampled impurity. While woman depends on
man for everything, man's love accepts, and his
generosity can never do enough to discharge the
delicious and sacred obligations; but let woman

enter into the ruder employments of life as man's rival, and she passes herself as a slave under those inexorable laws of trade which are without sex or sentiment. Perhaps in one branch of medicine there might appear a fitness in her claim to matriculation; but even in that branch, circumstances of sudden difficulty and danger were of every-day occurrence, requiring the steadier nerves, cooler judgment, and quicker action of a medical man to deal with. If asked for his sublimest ideal of what women should be in time of war, he would point to the dear women of his people as he had seen them during the recent struggle. The Spartan mother sent forth her boy bidding him return with honor—either carrying his shield, or on it. The women of the South sent forth their sons, directing them to return with victory; to return with wounds disabling them from further service, or never to return at all. All they had was flung into the contest—beauty, grace, passion, ornament; the exquisite frivolities so dear to the sex were cast aside; their songs, if they had any heart to sing, were patriotic; their trinkets were flung into the public crucible; the carpets from their floors were portioned out as blankets to the suffering soldiers of their cause; women bred to every refinement of luxury wore home-spuns made by their own hands; when materials for an army-balloon were wanted, the richest silk dresses were sent in, and there was only competition to secure their acceptance. As nurses of the sick, as encouragers and providers for the combatants, as angels of charity and mercy adopting as their own all children made orphans in defence of their homes, as patient and beautiful household deities, accepting every sacrifice with unconcern, and lightening the burdens of war by every art, blandishment, and labor proper to their sphere,—the dear women of his people deserved to take rank with the highest heroines of the grandest days of the greatest countries. Talking further upon woman, Mr. Davis stated his belief that when women prove unfaithful to their marriage vows, it will in almost every instance be found the husband's fault. Men throw their wives, or allow them to be thrown, into the companionship of male associates whom they know to be dissolute; neglect them, while the illicit lover pays every attention, and then grow angry at the result of their own criminal folly. It is either this, or that the man has chosen, without sufficient inquiry, a woman whose unfitness for the relations of wife might have been readily ascertained. No woman will err if treated properly by a husband worthy of the name; but she is the weaker vessel and must be protected.

CHAPTER XVIII.

Mr. Davis on Sensation News.—The Condition of the Negro.—Gen. Butler at Drury's Bluff.—Bishop Lynch and the Sisters of Charity.—A Story after the manner of President Lincoln.

SEPTEMBER 3D.—Called upon prisoner, accompanied by Captain Evans, 3d Pennsylvania Artillery, Officer of the Day. Had passed a comfortable night, the erysipelas again receding, and the carbuncle commencing to slough out. Reported to General Miles: "Prisoner Davis slightly better this morning." Still complained of the unwholesome atmosphere of his casemate, pointing to some crumbs of bread which he had thrown to the mouse only a day or two before, now covered with mould. Made no reply to this, not knowing what would be the action of the authorities on my recommendation, though hoping, and, indeed, fully trusting that it would be favorable.

Mr. Davis referred to some financial frauds in Wall Street, then exciting much attention in the Northern press, remarking that these insanities or

242

epidemics of financial and other kinds of crime appeared by some unknown law to follow every period of great political excitement. Perhaps the average of crime was at all times the same in every given population—as many eminent statisticians had maintained—the apparent increase of viciousness only arising from the fact that during the greater excitement, whatever that might be, we could spare no attention to minor matters, and now they struck us with a sense of novelty. The Northern press had been working with treble power and at fever-heat for some years, and would require another year to calm back into ordinary journalism. Sensationalism was the necessity at present, and offences which would have been dismissed with a paragraph in the police reports four or five years ago, were now magnified into columns or a page of startling capitals. The cruelty of dragging in family history and the names of relatives Mr. Davis dwelt upon, speaking with great sympathy of a venerable father whose grey hairs, heretofore without a blemish, were now sprinkled by the reports in Northern papers with the mire into which his son had fallen. With the criminal, and all his conscious aiders and abettors, the law and public opinion were entitled to deal;

but when journalism passed beyond this limit, and dragged before the gaze of unpitying millions the lacerated and innocent domestic victims of a son's or husband's crime, the act was so inhuman that to term it brutal would be to wrong the dumb creation. True, in tracing out and developing a crime, we had often to enter upon the otherwise sacred privacy of domestic relations; and if anything therein found could materially forward the ends of justice, the lesser right would have to be sacrificed to the greater. But the practice of dragging before the public the whole history of a criminal in his non-criminal relations—his wife and wife's family, his father and father's family, their manner of life, circle of friends, and so forth—deserved reprobation. It is the innocent and pure—and always in the exact measure of their purity and innocence—who most suffer from such offences as the one he was noticing. To the guilty man himself, unless hardened beyond reach of conscience, or dread of shame, the explosion which consigns him to prison must be a positive relief. The agony of anxiety is over; pride has suffered its benumbing shock, and the pain of its former protest is paralysed. In the solitude of his cell he is at peace, or in the companionship of the convict-yard there are none to mock his degradation. Mr. Davis spoke with great feeling on this matter, mentioning several cases which had come to his knowledge, and in particular the default of an army officer while he was Secretary of War. It had been a most painful case, for, up to the moment of the exploitation, he had been on terms of intimacy with the defaulter's family.

Speaking of army defaults, Mr. Davis remarked that our Government seemed to have trouble with the officers appointed to take care of the negroes. The better plan would be to remit their care and future to the several States. None could manage the black for his own good and the public interest so well as those who had been reared with them and knew their peculiarities. Once free, the necessities of labor and the laws of supply and demand would interfere to secure justice to the black laboring class, even were there any disposition to deny it, which he did not believe. Mr. Davis said, judging from the inevitable logic of the case and reports reaching him during the war, that the class of civilians who rushed South in the wake of our armies, professing intense philanthropy for the negro as their object, were about

the most unsafe class to whom the destinies of any
ignorant and helpless people, out of whom money
were to be made, could have been entrusted.
Men, the most pure and upright in previous life,
when suddenly given control of wealth for dis-
tribution to the ignorant and helpless, in too
many cases, if not the majority, will gravitate, by
force of protracted temptation, into corruption.
He instanced the dealings of the Department of
the Interior with the Indians—a hideous history,
for which the country should blush, though not a
little of the peculations and extortions practised
by our Indian Agents against the various tribes,
had been placed on record. Mr. Davis then spoke
of the various Indian nations with whom he had
been thrown in contact during his earlier life
when serving in the army, giving the habits and
leading characteristics of each, but with a rapidity
and fluency of Indian names which (the subject
being new to me) I could not follow. The general
spirit of his remarks was kind to the Red Man,
lamenting his wrongs, and the inevitable obliteration of his race as a sacrifice under the
Juggernaut of civilization.

Recurring to the management of the negroes by
professed philanthropic civilians of the North, Mr.

Davis said that all the best men of both sections were in the armies, and that these civilian camp-followers partook in their nature of the buzzards who were the camp-followers of the air. He said they reminded him of an anecdote told in Mississippi relative to a professed religionist of very avaricious temper, which ran as follows:

Driving to church one Sunday, the pious old gentleman saw a sheep foundered in a quagmire on one side of the road, and called John, his coachman, to halt and extricate the animal—he might be of value. John halted, entered the quagmire, endeavored to pull out the sheep; but found that fright, cold, damp, and exposure had so sickened the poor brute that its wool came out in fistfuls whenever pulled. With this dolorous news John returned to the carriage.

"Indeed, John. Is it good wool—valuable?"

"Fust class. Right smart good, Massa. Couldn't be better."

"It's a pity to lose the wool, John. You'd better go see; is it loose everywhere? Perhaps his sickness only makes it loose in parts."

John returned to the sheep, pulled all the wool, collected it in his arms, and returned to the carriage.

"It be's all done gone off, Massa. Every hair on him was just a fallin' when I picked 'um up."

"Well, throw it in here, John," replied the master, lifting up the curtain of his wagon. "Throw it in here, and now drive to church as fast as you can; I'm afraid we shall be late."

"But de poor sheep, massa," pleaded the sable driver. "Shan't dis chile go fotch him?"

"Oh, never mind him," returned the philanthropist, measuring the wool with his eye. "Even if you dragged him out, he could never recover, and his flesh would be good for nothing to the butchers."

So the sheep, stripped of his only covering, was left to die in the swamp, concluded Mr. Davis; and such will be the fate of the poor negroes entrusted to the philanthropic but avaricious Pharisees who now profess to hold them in special care.

I remarked that this story reminded me of Mr. Lincoln's happy way of arguing his own position, while not appearing to argue at all.

Mr. Davis said he had heard many of Mr. Lincoln's stories, or stories attributed to him, but knew not how much to believe. When a man once got a reputation of this sort, he was given credit for all the curious stories afloat; nor could he conceive how a man so oppressed with care as Mr. Lincoln, could have had any relish for such pleasantries. Recurring to the subject of the philanthropic guardians of the negro, he asked me, if ever released from duty in Fort Monroe—which he as selfishly hoped would not be until he also was released, either by order of man or the summons of death—to visit New England and count for myself how many doughty talkers for the negro, before the war, had worn sword on thigh or carried musket in hand during its continuance? For the agitators of the South, as they were called, this could be said: that they had veritably staked life, property, and honor in support of their ideas.

Of the negro race Mr. Davis spoke most kindly, saying that the irregularities into which they had been betrayed, arose from misinformation spread amongst them by these civilian philanthropists. They were taught that the General Government was about transferring to them in fee the estates of the Southern whites, thus enabling them to live in opulence and idleness (as they hoped) through all future time. Whatever might be the designs of the future, this had not yet been done; and hence the disappointment of the negroes, who began to regard freedom as a much less blessing than they at first supposed. They took their idea of freedom from what they had seen of their masters, and imagined that to be free—pure and simple—implied as a concomitant all the comforts and luxuries which they had seen their masters enjoying under the old system of labor. He was sorry for the poor negroes with his whole heart. The future might possibly better their condition—in the next generation, not in this; but to him, the freed slaves seemed like cage-bred birds enjoying their first hour of liberty, but certain to pay a terrible penalty for it when night and winter came, and they knew neither where to find food or shelter.

Mr. Davis said that we—himself and the writer —had once, from my account, been opposite each other in battle. It was on May the 16th, 1864, at the engagement which we called Drury's Bluff, but not properly so, the battle having its central point at the house of the Rev. Mr. Friend, and both its wings resting on Proctor's Creek. There were several lines of defence between that battle-ground and the works at Drury's Bluff. Beauregard had been fooling Butler for some days by skirmishing and falling back, in order to draw Butler on. Davis was present on the foggy morning of the decisive day—the day which rendered Butler permanently powerless for further evil, and hoped that morning to capture our entire army. This would have been done if General Whiting (I think) had obeyed orders. His orders were to flank Butler, while the battle was going on in front, and cut him off from his base and works at Bermuda Hundred. This might easily have been done, but the orders miscarried in some manner, and General Butler, with the 10th and 18th Corps, forming his force, escaped—though Mr. Davis heard we had hardly enough shovels in our army to bury the dead. General Terry, with the 10th Corps, had been allowed to carry their exterior line of rifle-pits. Then, Beauregard massed his forces, charged out of his works, cut the 18th Corps to pieces, and very badly crippled the 10th.

I replied that I remembered all the incidents of the day very well, having been nearly captured by some of his cavalry bushwhackers while endeavoring to take care of my wounded near Chester Station, on the railroad from Richmond to Petersburg. Nothing but letting them count the nails in the hindshoes of my horse had saved me. Returned about half an hour after that, and brought off my wounded without difficulty. Then related to Mr. Davis the incident of General Walker, of Beauregard's staff, which forms the introduction to this volume.

From this point the conversation diverged to the treatment of our wounded by the Confederate surgeons. I said that complaint had been made, and with justice, as I could personally certify in some cases, that unnecessary amputations had been performed on wounded Union soldiers falling into the hands of Confederate surgeons. Mr. Davis said this was undeniable; but not more so with our men than with the boys of his own people. They had been obliged to accept as surgeons in the Southern army many lads who had only half finished their education in Northern colleges. Besides, their facilities for transporting and taking care of the sick were greatly deficient; nor had they had proper hospital stores, nor appliances for cure, in any such abundance as with us. To bunglers in the art of surgery, or men too hurried for scientific treatment, amputation is always a readier remedy than the slow process of splints, removing daily dressings; and all he would claim on behalf of his surgeons was, that they had treated all the wounded, Confederate or Union, with impartiality; and that if too many amputations had been performed on the one, they had likewise been performed on the other. He then referred to the courtesy of the medical profession towards each other, as exhibited when surgeons had been taken prisoners. They were always treated on his side, and so far as he knew upon our side, with the respect due to scientific non-combatants, whose business was the healing, not the wounding, art. It was by these little humanities war endeavored to soften the natural brutalities of its nature to the educated mind.

Mentioned to Mr. Davis that I had once had a very interesting day's service exchanging some three or four hundred Confederates for about an equal number of our own wounded boys. Brigadier-General James F. Hall had been our officer of exchange, and Surgeon Bontecue my associate. We steamed up Charleston Harbor in the hospital-ship *Cosmopolitan*, and were met by Bishop Lynch on a vessel carrying our wounded. The Bishop had been extremely kind, receiving the blessings of our boys, who spoke in warm terms of his Christian humanity. So far as I could judge from that specimen, our wounded had not anything to complain of in their treatment—at least nothing which the necessities of their situation rendered avoidable. To this Mr. Davis replied in warm eulogy of Bishop Lynch, as also of the Sisters of Charity, not one of whom he could ever pass without raising his hat—an act of involuntary reverence. They had indeed been the silent angels of the war, carrying comfort and religious faith to every couch of suffering. Of what they had done, history might make no mention; but it would remain for ever engraven upon the hearts of the tens of thousands they had helped and comforted. Emblems of purity and mercy, no lives in the whole world could be more beautiful than theirs. Their hymns were an undertone or diapason of sacred melody through all the crash of arms and the harrowing chorus of groans. If it had been possible in his estimation to elevate the respect for woman, the conduct of the Sisters of Charity would have done so. Meeting Bishop Lynch casually one day, he asked him in the usual commonplace how the world went with him. Never should he forget—for it was but an echo from his own soul—the tone in which the Bishop replied, "This war, Mr. Davis; this war. I am heart-sick, heart-sick, heart-sick!"

CHAPTER XIX.

Treason.—State and National.—The Fish-Hawk and Bald-Eagle.—Mr. Davis on Senator Benton, Ex-President Buchanan, and President Andrew Johnson.—Preparations to remove Mr. Davis to Carroll Hall.

SEPTEMBER 6TH.—Called upon Mr. Davis once or twice, I remember, between the interval of my last date and this, but have lost notes. Called to-day, accompanied by Captain Titlow, 3d Pennsylvania Artillery, Officer of the Day, and found prisoner in a more comfortable state of mind and body than he had enjoyed for some days. Healthy granulations forming in the carbuncle.

Mr. Davis said the clamor about "treason" in our Northern newspapers was only an evidence how little our editors were qualified by education for their positions. None seemed to remember that treason to a State was possible, no less than to the United States; and between the horns of this dilemma there could be little choice. In the North, where the doctrine of State sovereignty was little preached or practised, this difficulty might not seem so great; but in the South a man had presented the unpleasant alternatives of being guilty of treason to his State when it went out of the Union, by remaining, what was called "loyal" to the Federal Government, or being guilty of treason to the General Government by remaining faithful to his State. These terms appeared to have little significance at the North, but were full of potency in the South, and had to be regarded in every political calculation.

Mr. Davis said he had been much interested all the morning watching from the grated embrasure, near which his bed lay, the free flight of fish-hawks, so plentiful during the summer in Hampton Roads, and some of which still lingered. The bird was a sacred guest, visiting the coast on particular days in every season, and carrying with its appearance the glad tidings to so many fishermen that the shoals of shad, alewives—mossbunkers he believed we called them in the North—and blue-fish, were upon the coast. The fish-hawk or osprey was associated with the bald-headed eagle in such intimate relations, that to describe the habits of the one, necessitated some description of the habits of the other.

The osprey or fish-hawk visited the coast in early spring, on the same day that the fish he had named made their appearance. It built its nest in some dead tree standing near a barn or house, long experience having assured it that it ran no danger from man. Its food was upon the deep; and from the farm it dwelt upon, the osprey took nothing but the support of a single decaying tree. Here it huddled together in the forks nearest the ground, a couple of cart-loads of twigs and branches to form its nest—sticks varying in thickness from a man's little finger to that of a cart-rung. On these were laid coatings of meadow-grass, and finally the feathers from its own breast, and so the nest was made and in it the eggs deposited. From this perch the fish-hawk mother kept a wary eye upon the waters, its male being close at hand, either to bring it food or protect the eggs or young during its absence. At the first ripple, betokening a shoal of fish in the distance, away sailed the male or female parent, poising over the surface of the waters on balanced wing until the fish—who had seen its shadow coming and struck .for the bottom— should reappear. Then it folded its wings and dropped down like a bullet, reëmerging presently with a shad, or blue-fish, ʹor alewife, varying in weight from half a pound to four pounds, clutched firmly in its talons—the head of the fish being always directly under its own head, which was not idle in picking out the eyes. Thus it sailed along the water for half a dozen yards until the grasp of its talons was made more secure; then suddenly rose on perpendicular wing in the air and struck off for its nest near the barn-yard.

But there is another bird on the coast, added Mr. Davis, for whom these fishing operations have much interest. It is the bald-eagle, who builds on some crag, if there be any crag within vision of the sea; and if not, in the tallest tree that he can find, and farthest from the haunts of men. As he sees the fish-hawk sail forth, the eagle rivets his far-piercing eyes on the bird's motions. Then, as the osprey rises with his prey, the eagle shakes out the broad vans of his wings, looks at them to see that every feather is in place, and sullenly swoops upward into the air with the assurance of a conqueror. There is a wild scream from the osprey as it endeavors to rise higher, not satisfied as yet but some other fish-hawk with its prize may be the eagle's quarry. A few moments more and the hunt is certain; the fish-hawk drops its prey, and flies out to sea with redoubled screams, while the grave eagle rapidly descends with unblinking eyelids upon the prize that has been dropped for his morning or noon repast, often seizing it before it strikes the ground or water, and proceeds to make a meal. "This is the history of these birds," concluded Mr. Davis, "and I have watched them with the most lively interest, though the circumscribed view from my inclosure gave me no means of observing more than the exploits of the gulls and fish-hawks in the capture of their prey."

This rule of prey and being preyed on, added Mr. Davis, appeared universal through nature. Up to the regal footstool of man, no beast, or bird, or fish, could be pointed out which did not prey on some minor creation of the animal or vegetable world, and was not preyed on in turn. Even with man, the stronger by nature preyed upon and absorbed the weaker; and this, though a harsh philosophy, was the sum and result of worldly experience. The terms virtue and vice were comparative, not absolute. The man of natural virtue might have no virtue at all. It is the man who restrains his passions when they are strongest, who is entitled to wear the crown.

Mr. Davis then quoted, though rarely quoting poetry, the well-known lines from Burns:—

> Who knows the heart—it's he alone,
>   Decidedly can try us ;
> He knows each chord—its various tone,
>   Each spring its various bias ;
> Then at the balance let's be mute,
>   We never can adjust it—
> What's done we partly may compute,
>   But know not what resisted.

A remark, that I hoped to see him soon resuming his walks on the ramparts, and reading less continually in a recumbent posture, called out several anecdotes from Mr. Davis relative to Senator Benton of Missouri, who was, he said, an incessant student, never quitting his room except in necessity, but taking all the exercise he thought needful with dumbbells and calisthenic exercises of his own choice. Senator Benton had one peculiarity very amusing to those who knew him, his desire to contradict and make a case against such of his associates as were about speaking on some point peculiarly within their own province of practical observation or education. Thus, if a Senator from California gave notice that on such a day he would introduce a resolution relative to gold-mining, or the Senator from Massachusetts gave similar notice relative to the fisheries, Mr. Benton would immediately bury himself in his library and commence coaching up, or "cramming," as it was called in college, for the forthcoming debate. He would read all varieties of books on the subject, arm himself with the most minute and comprehensive statistics, and thus intellectually equipped, take the field against whatever view the Senator who had given notice of the motion might advance. The result would be that a few home-thrusts from the lance of practical experience would bar all the delicate theories of Mr. Benton's authorities to shreds; but these debates were useful as giving the Senate a sketch of the two sides which every question has —that of theory and fact.

As Mr. Davis was speaking of the Senate, asked him his opinion of President Johnson to which for some moments he made no reply, apparently hesitating whether to speak on the subject or not. At length he said, that of President Johnson he knew no more than the papers told every one; but that of Mr. Johnson, when in the Senate, he would as freely speak as of any other member. There were, of course, differences between them, more especially just previous to the retirement of the Southern representatives from Congress. The postition of Mr. Johnson with his associates of the South had never been pleasant, not from any fault or superciliousness on their side, but solely due to the intense, almost morbidly sensitive, pride of Mr. Johnson. Sitting with associates, many of whom he knew pretended to aristocracy, Mr. Johnson seemed to set up before his own mind, and keep ever present with him, his democratic or plebeian origin as a bar to warm social relations. This pride—for it was the pride of having no pride—his associates long struggled to overcome, but without success. They respected Mr. Johnson's abilities, integrity, and greatly original force of character; but nothing could make him be, or seem to wish to feel at home in their society. Some casual word dropped in debate, though uttered without a thought of his existence, would seem to wound him to the quick, and again he would shrink back into the self-imposed isolation of his earlier and humbler life, as if to gain strength from touching his mother earth. In a word, while other members of the Senate were Democrats in theory or as to their political faith, Mr. Johnson was a Democrat of pride, conviction, and self-assertion—a man of the people, who not only desired no higher grade of classification, but could not be forced into its acceptance or retention when friendly efforts were made to that end. He was an immense worker and student, but always in the practicalities of life; little in the graces of literature. His habits were marked by temperance, industry, courage and unswerving perseverance; also, by inveterate prejudices or preconceptions on certain points, and these no arguments could shake. His faith in the judgment of the people was unlimited, and to their decision he was always ready to submit. One of the people by birth, he remained so by conviction, continually recurring to his origin, though he was by no means the only Senator of the South in like circumstances. Mr. Davis mentioned Aaron V. Brown, of Mississippi, who had been Postmaster-General under President Buchanan and several others, who were of like Democratic education with Mr. Johnson, but who seemed to forget, and in regard to whom it was forgotten by their associates, that they had ever held less social rank than that to which their talents and industry had raised them. Of Mr. Johnson's character justice was an eminent feature, though not uncoupled—as true justice rarely fails to be—with kindliness and generosity. He was eminently faithful to his word, and possessed a courage which took the form of angry resistance if urged to do, or not to do, anything which might clash with his convictions of duty. He was indifferent to money and careless of praise or censure when satisfied of the necessity of any line of action. But for his decided attitude against secession, he would probably have been given the place of Mr. Stephens on the Presidential ticket of the Confederacy. Mr. Stephens, indeed, held the same attitude up to the last moment; but on the secession of his State, had two alternatives of State or Federal "treason," as it was called, presented, and chose the latter.

Mr. Davis remarked that Mr. Buchanan more fulfilled the European ideal of a Chief-of-State in his social relations than any American since Washington. He was dignified, polished, reticent, and suave; fond of lady-gossip and the atmosphere of intrigue; a stickler for the ceremony of power. His misfortune was, as regarded his reputation North, that he could not forget in a month, and at the dictation of a party only representing the majority of one section, all those principles which had been imbibed in his youth and formed the guiding-stars of his career through over fifty years of public service. Of Mr. Cushing, of Massachusetts, Mr. Davis spoke in terms of praise, eulogizing his general talents, and more especially his soundness as an exponent of Constitutional law. He also referred to Mr. George M. Dallas as his model for the externals of a diplomatic representative, quoting something he had once known Mr. Cobden, of England, to say or write; in substance, that Dallas reminded him of some stately courtier-portrait in an old picture-gallery, suddenly clothing itself with flesh and stepping down from the wall to again pace with living men, while preserving all the passionless immobility of its pictorial experience.

After quitting prisoner, proceeded, by invitation of General Miles, and in company with that officer, to make an inspection of the fort, for the purpose of selecting more healthful quarters for the State prisoner. Decided that rooms in second story of the south end of Carroll Hall would best suit—a building long used as officers' quarters, near the main sally-port, and in which nearly every officer of the old army was for some months quartered after quitting West Point, and before being assigned to general duty elsewhere. It is a tradition in and around Old Point Comfort, that both Grant and Sherman occupied in their day the very chambers selected for the second incarceration of Mr. Davis. As with the case-mate, there were to be two rooms used for the prisoner's confinement. In the outer one a lieutenant and two soldiers were constantly stationed on guard, having a view of the interior chamber through a grated door. Opposite this door was a fireplace. To its right, when facing the door, a window heavily grated, and with a sentinel continually on duty before it, pacing up and down the piazza. Opposite the window a door leading into the corridor, but permanently fastened with heavy iron clamps, and in this door a sliding-panel in which the face of a sentinel was continually framed by night and day, ready to report to his officer the first sign of any attempt on the prisoner's part to shuffle off this mortal coil by any act of self-violence. It was of this face, with its unblinking eyes, that Mr. Davis so bitterly complained in after days; but this is anticipating. The prisoner, as was said of Lafayette, is perhaps "not sick enough yet," and has to suffer some further weeks of exposure in his present casemate.

The rooms being selected, General Miles gave orders to the Engineer Department for their speedy conversion from quarters to a prison, the piazza being prolongated and raised by a flight of stairs, so that access to the ramparts could be had by Mr. Davis without a descent to the ground-tier, which invariably caused a crowd to collect, with its usual unpleasant attendants of staring and whispering commentaries.

September 7th.—Called on Mr. Davis, accompanied by Captain Corlis, aide-de-camp to General Miles, Officer of the Day. Found the health of prisoner not differing from the preceding day, and so reported to the General commanding in the bulletin required of me at this time.

Told Mr. Davis, thinking it would cheer him and help to soothe his nervousness, that I had reason to hope he would soon be removed to more comfortable quarters. Was sorry for this afterwards, as the protracted and unforeseen delays in his removal only made him more painfully fretful in regard to the poisonous atmosphere of his present casemate. Had only a brief interview with Mr. Davis, there being much sickness in the fort then, and many demands upon my time. Mentioned that I thought in a few days of paying

Richmond a visit; General Alfred H. Terry, my old commander in the 10th Army Corps, having now his headquarters at that place. I had spent many days in front of the city as Chief Medical Officer of the 10th Corps, and Acting Medical Director of the Army of the James; had once caught a glimpse of the promised land from the Pisgah of a battery on the south-east, and about four miles removed, but had not then been permitted to enter. Mr. Davis pleasantly replied that if Richmond were my land of promise, the Caleb and Joshua visiting it would carry back but slender bunches of grapes. His people had suffered terrible privations, but with the severities and necessities of war removed, he hoped they would now be better supplied.

CHAPTER XX.

Visit to Richmond.—General Lee.—Mr. Davis on Horseback Exercise.—Macaulay's Pictorial Power.

SEPTEMBER 11TH.—Called on Mr. Davis, accompanied by Captain Bickly, 3d Pennsylvania Artillery, Officer of the Day. Found him convalescent in all respects, able to walk on the ramparts and in good spirits, considering his situation. Told him, as he was well, I was about starting that day for Richmond, to be gone about a week, and would be happy to carry any social messages he might wish to send any friends in that city. Mr. Davis asked me to call upon his former pastor, the Rev. Dr. Minnegerode, Rector of St. Paul's; also upon other friends, giving me their names, who would be glad to receive me. He requested me to make his afflictions in prison appear as light as possible, for they had sufficient troubles of their own without borrowing more from his misfortunes. He also said Richmond had been a very beautiful city in the days gone by; but what with years of military operations and the fire, he feared its appearance must now be sadly altered. "Oh, the anxious moments I have spent in that city!" exclaimed Mr. Davis. "Cares that none can understand who have not been called to fill the first positions of responsibility in revolutionary times. What hopes and fears, tried by enemies without and murmerers or mutineers within—though of the latter there were comparatively few. Taking all they suffered into view, my dear people stood firm and upheld my hands with a devotion and unanimity for which I can never be too grateful. God bless them, one and all, and grant them the sustaining influence of His grace!"

Mr. Davis spoke the last sentence with great fervor, his thin hands clasped, and tears brimming up in his eyes, though not allowed to run over. It was in such moments that his face, though not handsome, judged by any mere artistic standard, became very striking and noble in the delicate expression of its intellectual power and fervor.

Mr. Davis became solicitous for removal from his casemate, and wished to know when his new quarters in Carroll Hall would be ready? Would he be likely to be transferred there before my return? Told him I hoped to find him there on coming back, but could give no definite assurance —the engineers having to make some alterations in the rooms, and possibly some authorizing order being required from Washington.

To question of Mr. Davis, replied that Mr. Clay was far from well, extremely nervous, a prey to dyspepsia and want of sleep, but not in any immediate danger. Clay was my complaining patient, but Mr. Mitchel was a model of patience and good-humor, though terribly afflicted at times with asthmatic difficulties. Mr. Davis answered with a smile that Mitchel was used to it—had been in this or a worse strait before; but allowance must be made for himself and Clay, who were only serving their apprenticeship to Baron Trenck's profession. Took leave of prisoner, assuring him I would call on the friends he indicated in Richmond, deliver his messages of affectionate remembrance, and bring back all the social news.

September 22d.—Called on Mr. Davis for the first time since returning from Richmond, accompanied by Captain Titlow, 3d Pennsylvania Artillery, Officer of the Day. Found he had been inquiring for me several days, in consequence of suffering premonitory symptoms of a return of the erysipelas to his face. Reported his condition to Major-

General Miles, respectfully asking permission to call in Colonel Pineo, Medical Inspector of the Department, for consultation.

Mr. Davis inquired about friends in Richmond, asking, with a smile, was he still remembered there, or whether it had been found convenient to erase his name from the tablets of memory? Assured him that his friends appeared most solicitous for his welfare, especially the ladies, who had overwhelmed my wife with attentions during our brief visit, as the only means of expressing their gratitude for any alleviations of his situation which my duty as his medical attendant had imposed. Told him the destruction from the fire had been great, but in less than two years the city would have retrieved a prosperity not only equalling, but surpassing any it had yet known. Overlooking Richmond from the top of Gamble Hill, the clamor of trowels and hammers everywhere resounded beneath me, and it seemed like an enormous beehive, so incessant was the industry. Mentioned that General Terry, my old commander, had kindly placed the carriage of Mr. Davis at my disposal during the visit; and that I had visited with much interest, and not without sympathy the beautiful ground of Hollywood Cemetery where General J.

E. B. Stuart and so many other distinguished officers of the late Southern army now lie in graves, not nameless indeed, but as yet with no enduring monuments. Also spoke of having seen Mr. Lyons, Judge Ould, the Grants, and many other friends of his during my stay at the Ballard House.

Mr. Davis laughed about his carriage, and said that since some "Yankee" had to ride in it, he would prefer my doing so to another. During the war they had no time to build monuments to the illustrious dead—scarcely time enough or means enough to take care of the wounded living. If their cause had been successful, the gratitude of a new nation would have built splendid mausoleums and trophies to those who had lost their lives in founding it; but with the failure of the cause, this duty of piety and gratitude must now devolve on private associations of patriotic gratitude. General Jackson ("Stonewall") appeared to have some lively presentiment of death shortly before its occurrence, and had asked that his only monument might be a battle-flag hoisted over his grave until such time as the cause for which he fought was crowned with victory and secure from aggression. Speaking of a message of condolence and cheer the

Rev. D. Minnegerode had sent him, Mr. Davis spoke in warm terms of the learning, zeal, eloquence, fidelity, and Christian courage of that gentleman. General Lee had occupied a pew in the same church, and unless when absent unavoidably in the public service, was one of the most regular and devout attendants. General Lee was, undoubtedly, one of the greatest soldiers of the age, if not the very greatest of this or any other country; but had he drawn sword on the Federal side, must have been remitted to obscurity, under our system, in the first six months of the war. Nothing, however, shook the confidence of military men, competent to form a just opinion, in his superior qualifications for high command, and his career had nobly vindicated the calm estimate of professional judgment.

Mr. Davis inquired anxiously what signs there were, if any, of his removal to the new quarters I had mentioned before my Richmond visit? He was more than ever satisfied of the unhealthiness of his casemate, and the nights were now growing so chill, that one might as well be condemned to sleep in a stone coffin—a little better, for when the coffin comes the body has no feeling.

September 23d.—Called with Lieutenant A. H.

Bowerman, 3d Pennsylvania Artillery, Officer of
the Day. Found the condition of Mr. Davis not
materially changed, and so reported to General
Miles.

Prisoner renewed his questions about the proposed change in his place of confinement, begging
me, if I knew anything, even the worst, that he was
to be kept as now until death put an end to his
sufferings, not to conceal it from him any longer;
that suspense was more injurious to him than could
be the most painful certainty. Assured him that
I had no further information. A place had been
selected for his incarceration in Carroll Hall, the
requisite changes in the rooms made, and I heard
no reason for his non-transfer. If I did so, he
should be informed immediately.

Recurring to my Richmond visit, Mr. Davis
made many minute inquiries relative to former
friends, the apparent condition of the trades-
people in regard to prosperity, the social relations,
if any were allowed, between the occupying army
and the inhabitants. He said his people, having
done all their duty in war, had now the two duties
of forgetting the past, preparing to accept the
future. One of their great troubles in agricultural
districts must be the difficulty of getting draft

animals—horses, mules, and oxen having been so nearly swept away by the war. With nothing to regret in the past but its failure, the failure and its consequences should be accepted in good faith, and without a murmur. The future is always under the control of resolute men; and with industry and the influx of Northern and European capital, which must soon be tempted by the preabundant natural resources in the South, there could be no reason why national prosperity should not be fully re-established within half a dozen years—that is, if the Federal Government pursued a wise and generous course, allaying irritations, and diverting the minds of the people from their unsuccessful sacrifices, by pointing out and encouraging the splendid rewards of industry.

Mr. Davis renewed my attention to the steady deterioration of his health, which he regarded as chiefly due to the unfitness of his cell for a human habitation. His head had a continual humming in it, like the whizzing of a wound watch when its main-spring is suddenly broken. Little black motes slowly ascended and descended between his sight and whatever page he was reading, or object inspecting; and his memory likewise gave distinct indications of losing its elasticity. The carbuncle, however, was quite well, having left a deep-red cicatrice where it had been, precisely like the healed wound of a Minie bullet. Mr. Davis had not much flesh to lose on entering the fort; but believed he must have lost what little of it could be spared while still preserving life. Was glad to see from the papers that General Lee had accepted the presidency of Washington College, in Virginia. Happy would be the pupils who would grow up under the tutelage, and with the noble exemplar before them of his pure life, Christian faith, stainless integrity, and varied acquirements. The crying sin of our present educational system is a neglect of the moral nature, while overloading the intellectual with premature food, which it must be strained in digesting.

September 24th.—Called on Mr. Davis, accompanied by Captain Bickley, 3d Pennsylvania Artillery, Officer of the Day. Prisoner much better. The symptoms of a return of erysipelas gone. Had enjoyed his walk on the ramparts, and had seen a young lady on horseback who saluted him prettily as she passed. Did not know when raising his hat that he was bowing to his young hostess, but was informed she was my daughter, Anna. Remarked that she rode gracefully, sending her his compli-

ments, and then commented on the little attention
paid to horseback—the most healthful and delicious form of exercise—in the Northern States, and
more especially amongst the ladies, who from their
sedentary habits would derive most benefit from
its practice. When ladies unaccustomed to the
saddle did begin horseback, they had something
like a mania for fast cantering, or even galloping, it
being not only a pride but wonder to them at the
termination of each ride that they were still in their
seats. This was ungraceful, which should be a
sufficient bar to its continuance; it was also a
strain both on the rider and beast. A short burst
now and then along good parts of the road was very
well occasionally, to warm the horse and quicken
the rider's blood; but a gentle trot or rack was the
true gait for all who wished to derive health from
this exercise—more especially ladies; and yet the
canter or gallop was their favorite pace. The
Texan, Mexican, and Indian riders were among the
best he had ever seen; the men of these countries
—for the women never ride, except on journeys of
necessity, horseback as a pleasure or for health—
being several grades beyond their advance of civilization. Mr. Davis then spoke of Indians dis-
mounting and remounting while their ponies were

in full gallop, swinging their bodies down and picking up stones, etc.; but added there were none of these feats which he had not seen some of our dragoons do better and more certainly when once taught by the Indians. As a general rule, his people were better horsemen than those of the North. This was due partly to some remnant of cavalier origin in their education and sentiments, but still more to the distance between plantations, the want of good roads, and their devotion to agricultural pursuits. Their cavalry had been superior to ours in the commencement of the war for these reasons, but their stock of horses gave out sooner, and towards the close of the struggle it became difficult to mount a Confederate regiment, except by capturing a regiment of their enemies. General R. Stuart had been styled the Prince Regent of the South; but the name, as in many other cases, had not been to his advantage. He was a rarely gallant and noble gentleman, well supporting by his character the tradition that royal blood flowed in his veins. Subsisting his command gave him great difficulty—the cavalry having to be scattered for winter quarters in the Shenandoah valley, and other places more remote, where forage was plentiful, thus relaxing its discipline and bringing it already somewhat jaded into the field on the return of spring.

Mr. Davis then spoke of Macaulay's History of England with a freedom and unreservedness of admiration such as he rarely expressed. The portrait painting it contained was more vivid and subtle than anything on this side of Plutarch, and gave the surrounding circumstances to serve as a frame with broader scope and more liveliness of panoramic effect. The sketches of Clarendon, Shrewsbury, Marlborough, etc., etc., were not lifeless simulachre, but instinct with the turbulence and intrigues both of the social and political atmospheres in which they moved. No events of his actual life seemed more real than the life into which he was transferred by the absorbing power of Macaulay's genius. The portrait of Marlborough, Mr. Davis thought the great masterpiece of the work, though drawn with a pencil not sufficiently tempered by allowance for the unsettled, revolutionary, and conspiratorial times in which the scenes were laid.

CHAPTER XXI.

*Removal to Carroll Hall.—Some Curious Coinci-
dences.—A Foolish Precaution.—Interesting Letter from Mrs. Davis.—Adventures of the Family
from Incarceration of Mr. Davis up to date.*

OCTOBER 5TH.—Visited Mr. Davis once or twice in
the interval between this date and my last; but the
memoranda of such calls cannot be found. Remember, however, that the fort was visited during
the interval by Colonel Louis H. Pelouze, U. S. A.,
of the War Department—an able, kind, and gallant
young officer, whom I had previously known as
Assistant Adjutant-General of the Sherman expedition at Port Royal. Colonel Pelouze called for a
report of the health of the prisoner, with my opinion
as to the advisability or necessity of a change in his
place of confinement; visited the new quarters in
Carroll Hall, and directed General Miles—being
thereto empowered by his instructions—to remove
Mr. Davis from the casemate to his new and more
pleasant abode.

Called this day (October 5) with Captain Korte,
3d Pennsylvania Artillery, Officer of the Day, and
found Mr. Davis already looking much brighter,
exclaiming as I entered, "The world does move,

after all." The panel in the side-door opening on the corridor, in which a sentry's face was framed, gave him some annoyance, and he referred again to Lafayette in connection with the torture of a human eye constantly riveted on his movements. If his wish were to commit suicide, such a precaution would prove wholly unavailing. It looked rather as if the wish were to drive him to its commission. He then referred to some eminent French general, who, while a prisoner in England, procured and studied anatomical diagrams for the purpose of learning how life could be most certainly and painlessly lost, or with least disfigurement. He discovered that precise part of the breast in which the heart, unprotected by any rib, lay nearest the surface. Sticking a small pin through this spot in the diagram, he next applied the diagram to his breast, and marked, by a puncture, the exact place in which even the slight wound of a pin-prod would be fatal. Some time after, being transferred to France, and reincarcerated for a conspiracy against the life of the Emperor, he was found dead in his cell—the pin sticking in his heart, and the diagram, which he had never parted with, lying at his feet. This was an instance of how absurd it was to attempt preventing suicide by watchfulness. Even before being allowed knife or fork, there was no moment in which Mr. Davis could not have thrown down his burden of life, if wicked enough to have wished so rushing into the presence of his Creator.

Mr. Davis said his transfer to Carroll Hall had brought back many curious reminiscences of his past life. In the very building he now occupied, he had once, as Secretary of War, extended the prerogative of clemency to an officer, since eminently distinguished on the Federal side, who was before (or sentenced by) a court-martial under grave charges as an officer, though not affecting his honor as a man. The coincidences of life are very striking; of which he gave several curious examples, specially mentioning the simultaneous deaths of John Adams and Thomas Jefferson on the 4th of July, 1826, the half century anniversary of the Declaration of Independence, which had been so largely their joint work. Jefferson's only wish when failing was to live to that morning, on waking up to which his first exclamation was: "It is then Independence Day; Lord, now lettest thou thy servant depart in peace, for mine eyes have seen Thy salvation;" while the last words of Adams, his illustrious coadjutor, were: "It is a great and a good day—Jefferson yet survives." To many similarly strange coincidences Mr. Davis called my attention; but only those are preserved, though I vaguely remember his reciting some curious facts about the anniversaries of his birthday.

Mentioned to him that I had received an order

from General Miles, through Captain Church, that morning, directing "the meals for prisoner Davis to be furnished him punctually at $8\frac{1}{2}$ A. M., and 3 and 8 o'clock P. M., until further orders." These hours, I knew, did not suit his wishes or appetite, but of course must be accepted. He never ate more than two meals a day, and desired them more equably distributed.

Mr. Davis asked me some questions about the little young, big-headed, black boy, rechristened "Joe," though his true name was Thomas Bailey, who now carried over and delivered his meals. The boy was from the vicinity of Richmond, and had been for some time, with other members of his family, a refugee within our lines. It seemed natural to him to be so served, and the food came kindlier than from the hands of a soldier, though indeed, upon the whole, he had been most kindly and considerately treated by officers and men. Between the fighting men on both sides there was a generous and appreciative spirit; it was the rancorous non-belligerents of the different sections —they who had skulked the test of manhood— who would now prove most difficult to be appeased. What they lacked of honorable record during the progress of the struggle, they would endeavor to make up by ferocious zeal after the victory had been decided. The principle of compensation prevailed everywhere through nature; and for the

immense theoretical boon of freedom, with its
consequent incalculable destruction of property,
he feared his poor friends of "Joe's" race would
have to suffer fearfully in material privations and
an increased hostility of race.

Something—I cannot tell what, but probably the
constituents of his breakfast, for he was very fond
of fish—led Mr. Davis to speak of the manner in
which our fresh-water fish are disseminated; and
his views, though possibly old, were new to me and
of much interest. We are often astonished by
finding various breeds of fish appear in some
accidental cavity of the ground which was filled
with water; also, water-lilies and other aquatic
plants, though the new pond has no visible connection with any old pond supplied with such production. Mr. Davis explains this by supposing
that the quawk, poke, bittern, and the various
fresh-water ducks, play in the economy of nature's
pisciculture a part similar to that played by bees
and butterflies in the world of flowers. Bathing
and feeding in some older pond frequented by fish,
their feathers become impregnated with the fecun-
dated spawn, the seed of the water-lilies, and so
forth, and these are transferred to the new pond
on their first visit. The supposition of spawn
being sucked up into the clouds and descending in
rain was not worthy of regard, though so generally
accepted. If nothing else, the cold of the atmos-

phere at the height of the clouds would kill whatever animal life the spawn contained. The analogy of flower-life was entirely in favor of his explanation.

October 13*th*.—Called with Captain Theodore Price, 3d Pennsylvania Artillery, serving on the staff of Major-General Miles, Officer of the Day. Mr. Davis in good health, but complained of being treated as though he were a wild beast on exhibition, not a prisoner of state awaiting trial. Ladies and other friends of persons in authority at the fort, were let loose on the ramparts about the hour of his walk, to stare at him as though he were the caged monster of some travelling menagerie. He had endeavored to rebuke this during his last walk, when he saw a group of ladies waiting for his appearance, by turning short round and reëntering his cell. Dear and valuable as was the liberty of an hour's exercise in the open air, there were prices at which he could not consent to purchase it, and this was of the number. His general treatment Mr. Davis acknowledged to be good, though there were in it many annoyances of detail—such as the sentry's eye always fastened on his movements, and the supervision of his correspondence with his wife—unworthy of any country aspiring to magnanimity or greatness.

The following letter will be read with interest as giving a most graphic view of what the prisoner's wife and family had to endure from his quitting them on board the *Clyde*, in Hampton Roads, down to the day of its date; certain parts, reflecting upon individuals by name, I have taken the liberty to strike out, but the remainder of the letter is as written:

MILL VIEW (NEAR AUGUSTA, GA.), October 10, 1865.

COLONEL JOHN J. CRAVEN,

Chief Medical Officer, Fort Monroe, Va.

MY DEAR COLONEL:—Though you remain irrevocably dumb I am sure you hear me, and in addressing you feel as if writing to one of my oldest and most reliable friends. Every letter from my husband comes freighted with good wishes for you, and thanks for all your kindness to him in his hours of anguish and solitude. Can you doubt that my prayers for you, and appreciation of your goodness, have been even greater than his, for I could do nothing but pray? Mr. Davis sent me a carte de visite of your dear Anna, whose sweet face my baby knows and has been taught to kiss as her father's friend. The baby sends her a little fan, and a few white flowers, made in Augusta. I hope she may like them. Mr. Davis writes me that she has gone to the Moravian school, near Easton, where, I trust, our niece may have the pleasure of seeing her.

I am rendered very anxious by the obstinacy of

the erysipelas with my suffering husband. He complains—in answer to entreaties for an account of his condition without concealment—of a loss of sleep. I dread paralysis for him, his nerves have been so highly strung for years without relief. If you can, dear Doctor Craven, do entreat, and perhaps you may prevail upon the authorities to let him sleep without a light. He is too feeble to escape, and could not bear a light in his room when in strong health. The sequel of these attacks has always been an attack of amaurosis, and in one of them he lost his eye. It first came on with an attack of acute neuralgia; but it is useless for me to begin to tell you of his constitution. You must have seen pretty well its peculiarities, in the long and kind watches you have kept with him.

I had hoped to relieve his mind by a full letter of personal narrative, but that letter he has not received.   *   *   *   *   *

When he was taken from me on the ship, the provost-guard and some women detectives came on board, and after the women searched our persons, the men searched our baggage.

Either they or the soldiers standing around took everything they fancied, and some things so large that I did not see how their conduct could escape the eye of the guard, and of the officer who superintended the search. They then told my servants that they could go ashore, if they did not desire to go to Savannah. The husband of my negro nurse forced her to go, and the white girl left from an unwillingness to be exposed to a Southern climate. I entreated to be permitted to debark at Charleston, as my sister, Miss Howell, still continued to be ill, and I feared to return on the ship with a drunken purser, who had previously required Colonel Pritchard's authority to keep him in order; and going back, Mrs. Clay, my sister, and myself, would be the only women on the ship— but this was refused. Acting as my own chambermaid and nurse, and the nurse also of my sister and Mrs. Clay, who were both ill, we started for Savannah. We had a fearful gale, in which the upper decks once or twice dipped water, and no one could walk; but as I felt as wretched as could be, I did not fear a future state.

God protected us from the fury of the elements; but the soldiers now began to open and rob our trunks again. The crew, however, gave us some protection, and one of the officers in the engine-room gave up his cabin and locked everything we had left up in it. The Lieutenant of the 14th Maine, Mr. Grant, though a plain man, had the heart of a gentleman, and took care of us with the greatest assiduity. Some of the soldiers and crew helped me to nurse, and saved me many an hour of wakefulness and fatigue. My little daughter Maggie was quite like an old woman; she took her sister early every morning—for the nights were so rough I could not sleep, because it was necessary to hold the infant to avoid bruising it—and with the assistance of our faithful servant Robert, who held her still while she held her sister, she nursed her long enough for me to rest. Little Jeff and I did the housekeeping; it was a fair division of labor, and not unpleasant, as it displayed the good hearts of my children.

At the harbor of Charleston the sick began to improve. We procured ice and milk, and the day's rest, which the ship at anchor gave them, improved them much.

Arrived at Savannah we trudged up to the hotel quite in emigrant fashion, Margaret with the baby and Robert with the baggage; I, with Billy and Jeff and Maggie in quite an old-fashioned manner, keeping all straight and acting as parcel-carrier, for we could not procure any carriage and must walk until we reached the Pulaski House, where, after a day and night, we procured comfortable rooms. The innkeeper was a kind man, and felt for my unfortunate condition. He, therefore, did everything in his power to make us comfortable. A funny incident happened the day I arrived there.

A black waiter, upon answering my bell, and being told to call my man-servant Robert, replied very impertinently that "if he should see Robert he would give the order, but did not expect to see him." When Robert heard it, he waited till all the black servants had assembled at dinner, and then remarked that he should hate to believe there was a colored man so low as to insult a distressed woman; but if so, though a peaceable man, he should whip the first who did so. The guilty man began to excuse himself, whereupon Robert said: "Oh, it was you, was it? Well, you do look mean enough for that or anything else." From that time all the greatest assiduity could do was done for me, first from *esprit de corps,* and then from kind feeling.

The people of Savannah treated me with the greatest tenderness. Had I been a sister long absent and just returned to their home, I could have received no more tender welcome. Houses were thrown open to me, anything and everything was mine. My children had not much more than a change of clothing after all the parties who had us in charge had done lightening our baggage, so they gave the baby dresses, and the other little ones enough to change until I could buy or make more.

Unfortunately for me, General * * * * *, who, I hear, was "not to the manor born," was in command of the district at the time. I asked permission to see him, and as I was so unwell that I could not speak above my breath with a cold, and suffered from fever constantly—the result of exposure on the ship—I wrote to beg that he would come to see me, for his aide had told me the night before that I could not be permitted to leave Savannah, and having been robbed of nearly all my means, I could not afford to stay at the hotel; and, besides, as soon as I reached the hotel, detectives were placed to watch both me and my visitors, so I did not feel at liberty, thus accompanied, to go to private houses.

General * * * *'s aide, whose animus was probably irreproachable, but whose orthography was very bad, was directed to tell me that, except under very extraordinary circumstances, he did not go out of his office, and "all such" (which I afterwards found to mean myself) "as desired to see him would call at his office." To which I answered, that I thought illness and my circumstances constituted an extraordinary case; but that I was sorry to have asked anything which he "felt called upon so curtly to refuse," and requested to be informed what hour would please him on the following day, and I would do myself the honor to call upon him. Whereupon the same unfortunate, well-meaning, ill-spelling young gentleman wrote to me that "all such as desired might draw nigh from nine until three."

I went, accompanied by General Mercer of Savannah. Need I say that General * * * * did himself justice, and verified my preconceived opinion of him in our interview, in which he told me he "guessed I could not telegraph to Washington, write to the heads of Departments there, or to anybody, except through the regular channel approved;" and I could not write to my friends, "except through the Provost-Marshal's office;" and that I was permitted to pay my expenses, but must remain within the limits of Savannah.

With many thanks for this large liberty accorded so graciously, I bowed myself out, first having declined to get soldiers' rations by application for them to this government.

In this condition I remained for many weeks, until, fortunately for me, General Birge relieved him; who had it not in his power, however, to remove the restrictions any further than to take the detectives away, of whom I heard, but did not see. But General Birge permitted me to write unrestrictedly to whom I pleased, and appeared anxious, in the true spirit of a gentleman, to offer all the courtesies he consistently could.

My baby caught the whooping-cough, and was ill almost unto death for some days with the fever which precedes the cough; and then she slowly declined. I did what I could to give her fresh air; but the heat was so intense, the insects so annoying, and two rooms such close quarters, that she and I suffered much more than I hope you or yours will ever know by experience.

My most acute agony arose from the publication and republication in the Savannah *Republican* of the shackling scene in Mr. Davis's casemate, which, to think of, stops my heart's vibration. It was piteous to hear the little children pray at their grace, "That the Lord would give father something which he could eat, and keep him strong, and bring him back to us with his good senses, to his little children, for Christ's sake;" and nearly every day during the hardest, bitterest of his imprisonment, our little child Maggie had to quit the table to dry her tears after this grace, which was of her own composition.

I believe, Doctor, I should have lost my senses if these severities had been persevered in, for I could neither eat nor sleep for a week; but opiates, and the information of the change effected by your advice, relieved me; and I have thanked God nightly for your brave humanity. It is easier to fight with a revolver than to repeat unpleasant truths to a hostile and untrammelled power in the full indulgence of its cruel instincts. All honor to the brave men who fearlessly did so.

Though I ate, slept, and lived in my room, rarely or never going out in the day, and only walking out late at night, with Robert for protection, I could not keep my little ones so closely confined. Little Jeff and Billy went out on the street to play, and there Jeff was constantly told that he was rich; that his father had "stolen eight millions," etc. Billy was taught to sing, "We'll hang Jeff Davis on a sour apple-tree," by giving him a reward when he did so; and he made such good friends with the soldiers, that the poor child seemed to forget a great deal of his regard for his father. The little thing finally told me one day, "You thinks I'se somebody; so is you; so is father; but you is not; so is not any of us, but me. I am a Yankee every time." The rough soldiers, doubtless, meant to be kind, but such things wound me to the quick. They took him and made him snatch apples off the stalls, if Robert lost sight of him for a moment.

Finally, two women from Maine contemplated whipping him, because they found out that he was his father's son; but "a man more wise did them surprise," and took him off just in time to avoid a very painful scene to them as well as to me. These things went on in the street—I refer only to the street teachings—though these women were, with one other, dishonorable exceptions to the ladies in the house, until Captain * * * was ordered to Savannah on duty. He brought with him a person who I heard was his wife. As I never went into the parlor I did not see her, but my little son Jeff went accidentally into the room one day and interrupted a conversation she was indulging herself in with one of the negro waiters, in which she was laying down "the proper policy to be pursued towards Mr. Davis."

The servant, having been brought up by a lady, felt very uncomfortable, and said, "Madam, there is his son." She called little Jeff up to her and told him his father was "a rogue, a liar, an assassin, and that means a murderer, boy; and I hope he may be tied to a stake and burned a little bit at a time with light-wood knots. God forbid you should grow up a comfort to your mother. Remember, you can never be a gentleman while this country lasts. Your father will soon be hanged, but that death is too quick."

The negro retired mortified, and sent my nurse to call little Jeff; and so, with his little face purple with mortification, and wet with tears from his streaming eyes, he came up to me, leaving the pious and patriotic lady to find another audience as congenial to her tastes as the first had been.

I commended Jeff's gentlemanly conduct in making no reply; cautioned him against ever persecuting, or distressing a woman, or a friend, if it took that shape; made application for permission the next day to go away to Augusta; was refused, and then prepared the children to go where they would not see such indignantly patriotic and prophetic females. Nothing, however, but the dread of intruding into a secret and sacred grief prevented my writing poor Captain * * * a sympathetic note, to condole with him upon the dispensation of Providence under which, in the person of his wife, he groaned.

Hourly scenes of violence were going on in the street, and not reported, between the whites and blacks, and I felt that the children's lives were not safe. During General * * * 's *regime,* a negro sentinel levelled his gun at my little daughter to shoot her for calling him "uncle." I could mourn with hope if my children lived, but what was to become of me if I was deprived of them? So I sent them off with many prayers and tears, but confident of the wisdom of the decision. On the ship I understood a man was very abusive in their hearing of Mr. Davis, when my faithful servant Robert inquired with great interest, "Then you tell me I am your equal? You put me alongside of you in everything?" The man said "Certainly." "Then," said Robert, "take this from your equal," and knocked him down. The captain was appealed to, and upon a hearing of the case, justified Robert, and required an apology of the levelled leveller.

Little Jeff is now at the endowed grammar-school, near Montreal, in charge of a Mrs. Morris, who has the care of ten little boys of good family, some of them Southern boys, and is happy, so he writes me. Mrs. Morris superintends his clothes and person, and teaches him his lessons. She was chosen by the faculty of the college for her high character. Maggie is at the Convent of the Sacred Heart, in the same place, where Gen. William Preston's little girls are, and very kind they are to her. A nun is always present with the small girls, who are separated from the large girls. Little Billy is his grandmother's one pet and idol, always with her, and in pretty good health. I have sent their dear father a picture of Maggie's school, and a little scribbled letter from his big boy to me.

As soon as the dear children were gone, I hoped with my little weak baby (you see I am very honest with you) to make my escape out of the country to them; but when, upon coming to Augusta—which General Steadman gave me leave to do immediately upon his accession to command, through the very kind intercession of General Brannen, who succeeded General Birge—I was informed by a gentleman who said he had been told so authoritatively, that "if I ever quitted the country under any possible object, I would—no matter what befell Mr. Davis—never be allowed to return." I abandoned the intention. As might makes right in my case, and as my sister's health had failed rapidly in the South, and as she is a girl of rare judgment and good feeling, I sent her with my nephew to New York *en route* for Canada to take care of my devoted mother, who is now too old and delicate to be left alone.

My two nephews joined me here about a month ago and desired to take me home with them; but finding that the length of my tether only permitted me to browse "in Georgia," they stayed two days and were then forced to go home to their families. My baby has grown fat and rosy as the "Glory of France:" a rose which Mr. Davis recollects near the gate of our home. Under the kind treatment I have received, the fine country air (five miles from Augusta) and the privacy, I have also grown very much better; can sleep and eat, and begin to feel alive again with the frosty air, and loving words, and letters which meet me here as in Savannah.

Mr. Geo. Scheley is my host, and never had a child in her father's home a warmer welcome. I am at no expense, and entirely gladly welcome. The little baby eats hominy and drinks fresh milk; grows in grace and weight; talks a little, and being more gentle than little Jeff's friend, Mrs. * * * *, is a great pet with all. The difficulty is to accept all the invitations I get, or to refuse them rather— the whole Southern country teeming with homes, the doors of which open wide to receive me; and people are so loving, talk with such streaming eyes and broken voices of him who is so precious to them and to me, that I cannot realize I do not know them intimately. Mr. Davis should dismiss all fears for me. Money is urged upon me—everything. I only suffer for him. I do not meet a young man who fails to put himself at my disposal to go anywhere for me. I cannot pay a doctor's bill, or buy of an apothecary. "All these things are added unto me."

If I have written you too long a letter, my dear sir, it is because I have not collected my facts, but sought "quid scribam, non quem ad modum." Please give your good wife as much gratitude as she will receive from me; and I cannot permit you to measure it for yourself. My children shall rise up and call her blessed. May God show her and hers that mercy which you have been the means of bringing to my poor husband, and you will be blessed indeed. This is the constant prayer of your grateful friend.

VARINA DAVIS.

CHAPTER XXII.

A New Regiment on Guard.—Ordered not to Communicate with Mr. Davis, save on "Strictly Professional Matters."—The Correspondence about Prisoner's Overcoat.

OCTOBER 20TH.—Called on Mr. Davis, accompanied by Captain Titlow, 3d Pennsylvania Artillery, Officer of the Day. His health appeared satisfactory, and his change of quarters had already been of evident benefit.

Some remarks in the papers led him to say, that nothing could be more unjust than to accuse the South of having wished the destruction of the Constitutional Union of the States. It was not amongst his people that the Constitution had been continually denounced as a "bond with death and covenant with hell." To them the government had invariably been described as the "most beneficent and just government upon the face of the earth;" and it was only when what they regarded as a sectional Presidential ticket had been elected, and their rights of liberty and property threatened, that they rose to vindicate the reserved rights of State sovereignty, under a constitution which they believed to have been subverted.

Speaking of Mr. Bancroft, whose history of the

United States he much read and admired, frequently marking passages of it with his finger-nail, as a pencil was denied him, Mr. Davis said it was appalling to contemplate the extra labors which must be imposed on future historians by the increased activity of the press in these latter days, and the looseness with which their reports were made. It will require the labors of several lives to make the mere sifting of materials from the columns of the press, unless the historian shall boldly go to work by discarding all such authorities, and confining his scrutiny to the official reports on either side. He was glad to see that the various provisional State governments of the South were accepting the reconstruction policy of President Johnson, practically and in good faith. Universal amnesty—though he did not ask it for himself—with restoration of property and civil rights to all willing to take the oath of allegiance, would speedily restore to the whole country so much of harmony and homogeneity as was now possible, and so much needed by its political and financial interests. No apprehensions need be felt from any war with England or France, unless the South should be permanently alienated by despair of tolerant terms. Even then, as an American with no other country left him, he would be for unanimous support of the country against its European enemies, but the same sentiments might not be likely to prevail amongst the masses of his people. They had in their blood the faults of a Southern sky, "sudden and quick in quarrel, jealous of honor." The question of negro soldiers was not a new one in this war. Such class of soldiers had twice before been enlisted in the history of the country, but not trusted upon active service on either occasion; and when he had been in the War Department, a proposition had been urged by several eminent officers of the regular army for garrisoning the defences of the Southern coast with regiments of blacks, on the ground that they could resist the exposures of the climate better.

October 25th.—Called upon Mr. Davis, accompanied by Captain Korte, 3d Pennsylvania Artillery, Officer of the Day. Mr. Davis had been for some time complaining that his light suit of grey tweed was too thin for the increasing cold of the days on the ramparts of the fortress, and finding that his measure was with a tailor in Washington, I requested a friend of mine to call there and order a good heavy black pilot-cloth overcoat for the prisoner, and that the bill should be sent to me. Also, ordered from a store in New York some heavy flannels to make Mr. Davis comfortable for the winter. These acts, to me appearing innocent, and even laudable, caused great trouble, as may be seen by the following correspondence, finally leading to a peremptory order which almost altogether broke off the previously free relations I had exercised with Mr. Davis. This, however, will more properly appear further on, when the various letters on the subject are inserted under their proper date.

October 29th.—Called, accompanied by Captain R. W. Bickley, 3d Pennsylvania Artillery, Officer of the Day, who announced that his regiment was under orders to quit the fort on the last day of the month, preparatory to being mustered out of the service. Mr. Davis replied with much feeling, expressing his regret that a regiment whose officers had shown him so much genuine kindness within the limits of their duty, and whom he had come to regard more as friends than custodians, should be about quitting him—though he had no doubt of being treated with equal consideration by the officers of the incoming regiment, the 5th United States Artillery, with many of whose officers he had been acquainted before the war. To a prisoner new faces were never pleasant, unless the old faces had become intolerable from cruelty, which had been the reverse of this in his case. No matter what his fate might be in the future, he could never forget the 3d Pennsylvania Artillery.

Mr. Davis also referred to the kindness of Captain Grisson, of the staff of General Miles, in regard to a little matter which, though trivial in itself, had given him much annoyance. It arose in this manner: he had requested a barber to be sent to him, as his hair was growing too long. Captain Grisson brought a hair-dresser, but on the termination of the operation said it was the order of General Miles that the lopped hair should be carried over to head-quarters. To this Mr. Davis objected, first from having a horror of having such trophies or "relics" paraded around the country, and secondly because he wished to send it to Mrs. Davis; this latter probably an excuse to avoid the former disagreeable alternative. Captain Grisson replied that his orders were peremptory, but if Mr. Davis would fold the hair up in a newspaper and leave it on a designated shelf in the casemate, the Captain would step over to headquarters, report the prisoner's objections, and ask for further orders. This was done, and Captain Grisson soon returned with the glad tidings that the desire to obtain possession of these "interesting relics" had been abandoned. Mr. Davis also spoke with great interest of a volume called the Schonburgh Cotta Family, which had been sent for his perusal by a lady in Richmond. It had been brought, I believe, by the Rev. Mr. Minnegerode, when that gentleman called at Fort Monroe on the day of my return from Richmond to administer the Sacrament to his former parishioner.

October 31st.—Called with Captain Titlow, Officer of the Day, the last officer of the 3d Pennsylvania Artillery, who had charge of the prisoner. Mr.

Davis renewed his friendly and grateful messages to the officers of the regiment, specifying several by name, and desiring to be remembered by them. As it stormed, there had been a fire built in the grate, and Mr. Davis spoke of its cheering effect both on body, eye, and mind, the stove being both injurious and unpleasant, as it concealed the best part of the fire, which was its rich, homelike, and enlivening appearance. It had always appeared natural to him that savage nations, in the absence of revealed religion, should adopt fire as their god. It was the nearest approach in the material world to the invisible spirit of life. Negroes and Indians, even in summer-time, would build a fire and squat down around it, forgetting all the demands of labor and amusement. Indeed, one of the earliest instincts of humanity, whether civilized or savage, was to collect around a bonfire in our childhood.

The change to Carroll Hall had been of the greatest benefit to the prisoner's health, the air being purer as it was loftier, his own room more cheerful, and only subject to the drawback that he had human eyes from three directions continually fixed upon him through the grated door entering his room, the window opening on the piazza at his left, and the door opposite the window, with an open panel in it, opposite which stood a sentry.

November 1st.—Called with Brevet-Captain Valentine H. Stone, 5th U. S. Artillery, First Officer of the Day, from the new regiment garrisoning the fort. Mr. Davis appeared out of sorts—not body sick, but heart-sick, as he said himself. He appeared to scrutinize Captain Stone with great care, asking him all about his term of service, his early education, etc., as if anxious to find out everything ascertainable about the new men into whose hands he had fallen—an operation repeated with each new Officer of the Day who called to see him. Indeed this habit of analysis appeared universal with the prisoner. It seemed as if he put into a crucible each fresh development of humanity that crossed his path, testing it therein for as long as the interview lasted, and then carefully inspecting the ingot which was left as the result. That ingot, whether appearing to him pure gold or baser metal, never lost its character to his mind from any subsequent acquaintance. He never changed his opinion of a man, or so rarely as merely to prove the rule by its exception; and this was one of the faults alleged against him as a leader by his opponents. It may have been pride that would not abandon a judgment once formed; or, more probably, that Mr. Davis had been taught by his experience of the world, how rarely we improve the correctness of such estimates by subsequent alterations. In our first judgment, it is the nearly infallible voice of instinct, unbiassed by any other causes, which delivers the verdict; while in closer acquaintance afterwards, the acts of the hypocrite, or the familiarity which so blunts and deadens our perceptions, may interfere to lead us astray.

Mr. Davis said it was scandalous that government should allow General Miles to review his letters to his wife. They had to pass through the hands of Attorney-General Speed, who should be a quite competent judge of offensive matter, or what was deemed offensive. General Miles had returned to him several pages of a letter written to Mrs. Davis, containing only a description of his new prison in answer to her inquiries, the General declaring such description to be objectionable, perhaps suspecting that if told where he was confined, Mrs. Davis would storm the fort and rescue him *vi et armis*. This was both absurd and cruel—one of those acts of petty tyranny which was without excuse, because without any sufficient object. In regard to attempts at escape, General Miles might give himself no uneasiness. Mr. Davis desired a trial both for himself and cause, and if all the doors and gates of the fort were thrown open he would not leave. If anywhere in the South the Confederate cause yet lived, the thing would be different; but as that cause was now wrapped in the shroud of a military defeat, the only duty left to him—his only remaining object—was to vindicate the action of his people, and his own action as their representative, by a fair and public trial.

November 10th.—This day, in consequence of reports in some of the papers that an overcoat had been ordered for Mr. Davis from Mr. S. W. Owen, his former tailor, doing business at Washington, and a further report that I had been the medium for ordering it, the following letter was sent to me:

Headquarters, Military District of Fort Monroe, } Fort Monroe, Va., November 18, 1865. }

SIR:—The Major-General commanding directs me to inquire of you if any orders have been given by you, or through you, for an overcoat for Jefferson Davis?

Such a report has appeared in the papers.

Very respectfully, A. V. HITCHCOCK,

Captain and Provost Marshal.

To which, on the same date, I returned the following answer:

Office of Post Surgeon, Fort Monroe, Va., } November 10, 1865. }

CAPTAIN:—I have received the communication dated November 10th, Headquarters Military District, Fort Monroe, in which the Major-General commanding, directs you to inquire if any orders have been given by me, or through me, for an overcoat for Jefferson Davis.

In reply, I would respectfully state that I did order a thick overcoat, woollen drawers, and under-shirts for Jefferson Davis. I found as the cold weather approached he needed thick garments, the prisoner being feeble in health, and the winds of the coast cold and piercing.

I have the honor to be,

Very respectfully, your obedient servant,

(Signed) JOHN J. CRAVEN.

B'vt Lieut.-Col., Surg. U.S.V.

Capt. A. O. HITCHCOCK, A. D. C.

That any objection to my action in the matter should have been made, was about the last thing I should have expected—the prisoner's health being under my charge, and warm clothing for cold weather being obviously one of the first necessities to a patient in so feeble a condition. Let me add, that Mr. Davis had never asked for the warm clothing I deemed requisite, and that sending for it, and insisting upon its acceptance, had been with me a purely professional act. In the valise belonging to Mr. Davis, which was kept at the headquarters of General Miles, no heavy clothing could be found, merely containing a few articles of apparel chiefly designed for the warm climate of the South. General Miles, however, took a different view of my action, to judge from the following letter:

Headquarters, Military District, Fort Monroe, Va., }
Fort Monroe, Va., November 18, 1865. }

COLONEL:—The Major-General commanding directs that, in future, you give no orders for Jefferson Davis, without first communicating with these Head Districts.

Also, that in future, your conversations with him will be confined strictly to professional matters, and that you comply with the instructions regarding the meals to be furnished to prisoners Davis and Clay, and have them delivered more promptly. Also, report the price paid for Mr. Davis's overcoat, and by whom paid.

A. O. HITCHCOCK,
Capt. and A.D.C.

B'vt Lieut.-Col. J. J. CRAVEN, Post Surgeon.

This order I then regarded as cruel and unnecessary, nor has subsequent reflection changed my opinion. The meals for Mr. Davis I had sent at hours to suit his former habits and present desires —two meals a day at such time as he felt most appetite. I was now ordered to send his meals three times a day, and at hours which did not meet his wishes, and were very inconvenient to my family, his meals being invariably sent over at the same hour I had mine. The order to abstain from anything but professional conversation was a yet greater medical hardship, as to a man in the nervous condition of Mr. Davis, a friend with whom he feels free to converse is a valuable relief from the moodiness of silent reflection. The orders, however, I felt bound to accept and carry out in good faith; and hence, from this point, my memoir must unavoidably lose much of its interest. The next step in this difficulty will be seen in my annexed letter, dated the day following the receipt of my last communication from General Miles:

CAPT. A. O. HITCHCOCK, A. D. C.:

CAPTAIN:—I have the honor to acknowledge the receipt of your communication dated Headquarters, Military District, Fort Monroe, Va., Nov. 18, 1865; and in answer to your inquiry concerning the cost of the coat ordered by me for Mr. Davis, I would say:

That I do not know the cost of the coat; I have not yet received the bill. As soon as received, I

will forward it to the Major-General commanding.
I do not know that any person paid for the coat,
having directed that the bill should be sent to me
when ordering it.

I remain, Captain, very respectfully,

JOHN J. CRAVEN,

B'vt Lieut.-Col. and Post Surg. and Chief Medical Officer,

Military District, Fort Monroe, Va.

The next day—on the 20th, though dated the
17th—I received from Mr. Owen the sub-note in
reply, as will be seen, to a letter of inquiry addressed to him some nine or ten days previously:

DR. J. J. CRAVEN, U. S. A.,

Chief Medical Director,

Fortress Monroe, Va.:

DEAR SIR:—In reply to your favor of the 14th
inst., I would say the price of the coat sent you was
$125; and as regards the question you ask about
who paid for the coat, parties called at the store
and desired to pay for it. Not knowing your wish
on that subject, the money was left here until such
time as I should hear from you about payment
for it.

Yours respectfully,

(Signed) S. W. OWEN,

Per RUSSELL.

To conclude this correspondence, the two following letters will explain themselves:

Headquarters, Mil. Dist., Fort Monroe, Va.,
December 14, 1865.

B'vt Lt.-Col. J. J. CRAVEN,
Surgeon U. S. V.:

SIR:—The General commanding directs me to ask if the overcoat furnished the prisoner Davis has been paid for.

I am, very respectfully,
Your obedient servant,
JOHN S. McEWAN,
Capt., A. D. C., and A. A. A. G.

FORT MONROE, VA., December 15, 1865.

CAPT. JOHN S. McEWAN,
A. D. C., and A. A. A. G.:

SIR:—I have the honor to acknowledge the receipt of your communication, bearing date December 14th, 1865, stating that the Major-General commanding directs you to ask if the overcoat furnished Jefferson Davis has been paid for. In reply, I would respectfully state, that parties, without my approval, knowledge, or consent, called upon S. W. Owen, the tailor, interfered and interested themselves in the coat, leaving on deposit the price for the same. Seeing the coat was unlike the one I had ordered (a plain, black, pilot overcoat), I interested myself no further in the matter, leaving Owen, the tailor, to receive or refuse the money as he saw fit. He has received no money from me, neither did I authorize him to receive the pay for the overcoat from another.

I am, sir, very respectfully,
Your obedient servant,
JOHN J. CRAVEN,
Brevet Lieut.-Col., Surg. U. S. V., and Post Surgeon.

CHAPTER XXIII.

*General Summary in Conclusion.—The Character of
Mr. Davis.—Let us be Merciful!*

AND now my diary of a most interesting patient
ceases, for under the orders dated November 18th,
contained in the close of the preceding chapter, I
could hold no conversation with him except on
"strictly professional matters," up to the date of
my being relieved from duty at the fort, which took
place near the end of December, 1865, and these
would be of no interest to the public, even were I
at liberty to reveal them. Mr. Davis occasionally
suffered in health during the last month of my remaining his medical attendant, but the history of his
trifling ailments *per se,* and unrelieved by any conversation, would not form either a pleasant or amusing record. With the officers of the 5th U. S.
Artillery, as with his previous friends of the 3d
Pennsylvania, he continued to have most agreeable
relations—Major Charles P. Muhlenburgh, Captain
S. A. Day, and many others, displaying both generosity and consideration in their treatment of the
distinguished captive. Indeed, it was a remark
which must have been forced on every observer,
both during the war and since, that it is amongst
the non-belligerents of the North—the men, one
would think, with least cause to hate or oppress
our recent Southern enemies—that we must look

for those who appear actuated by the most vindictive feelings.

It was not my intention to have published this narrative until after the trial of the prisoner; but on submitting the matter to friends, whose judgment I relied upon, it was decided that there was no material in these pages which could bias or improperly interfere with public opinion, or the due course of justice. It must be remembered that during the past year Mr. Davis has lain a silent prisoner in one of our strongest forts, unable to reply by so much as a word to the myriad assaults which have been made both on his private character and public course. This is absolutely the first statement in his favor—if so it can be regarded—which the Northern press has yet given to the world; and the case against that prisoner must indeed be weak which cannot bear allowing a single voice to be raised in his defence, while seven-eighths of the Northern journals have been industriously engaged in manufacturing public sentiment to his injury. I know my notes are very imperfect—that I have lost much which would have been valuable to history; but such brief memoirs as I made were not originally intended for publication, but for my own pleasure or instruction, and that of my family; and it has been my conscientious effort to report him as he was, neither inventing any new sentiments to put in his mouth, or suppressing any material views on public questions which appeared in my note-book.

In many of the important political conversations, let me add, the words are as nearly as possible the exact language used by Mr. Davis, my memoranda upon such matters having been made as full as possible.

His self-control was the feature of his character, knowing that his temper had been high and proud, which most struck me during my attendance. His reticence was remarked on subjects where he knew we must differ; and though occasionally speaking with freedom of slavery, it was as a philosopher rather than as a politician—rather as a friend to the negro, and one sorry for his inevitable fate in the future, than with rancour or acrimony against those opponents of the institution whom he persisted in regarding as responsible for the war, with all its attendant horrors and sacrifices. Of the "abolitionists," as such, he never spoke, though often of the anti-slavery sentiment; and he impressed me as having in good faith accepted the new order of things which the late struggle and its suppression have made necessary.

The Southern States have been essentially conquered by military force, and now—taking the worst view of the case—await such terms as the conqueror may see fit to impose. The problem before all good men in the country—that for which our soldiers and sailors poured out their blood, and all loyal men labored and made sacrifices in their respective spheres—is the restoration of the Union as it existed in harmony, glory, and prosperity before the recent war, with, of course, such changes and modifications as the rebellion may have proved necessary. The writer believes it will be found that the men who were chief actors in the late rebellion, are now the promptest and most clear-headed in accepting its results; and are not only willing but solicitous to accept and forward all such changes as the new order of things may render requisite; passing a sponge over the political errors of the past, and now only aiming to direct their people in the road by which the material prosperity and glory of the Union, one and undivisible, may be most quickly secured for the benefit of all interests and sections.

Mr. Davis is remarkable for the kindliness of his nature and fidelity to friends. Of none of God's creatures does he seem to wish or speak unkindly; and the same fault found with Mr. Lincoln—unwillingness to sanction the military severities essential to maintain discipline—is the fault I have heard most strongly urged against Mr. Davis.

As for the rest, the character of Mr. Davis, we believe, will receive justice in history. Mistaken in devotion to a theory of State sovereignty, which, before the recent war, was all but universally accepted by the people of both sections, he engaged reluctantly (as he says) in a rebellion for the sustainment of his faith. He and those who thought and acted with him have suffered terribly for that error; but it can be neither magnanimity nor wisdom to slander or oppress them in their moment of misfortune. It is by the conciliatory and generous policy of President Andrew Johnson that the bleeding gashes of the body politic are to be bound up and healed; and in a restoration of the Union as it existed before the late sad conflict —with only slavery abolished, the rebel debt repudiated, and the national debt accepted in good faith—the aspirations of those who served in our army and navy will be most happily realized. If Mr. Davis has been guilty of any private crime, such as connivance with the assassination of Mr. Lincoln or authorized cruelties to our prisoners, no punishment can be too heavy for him; but let the fact of his guilt be established in fair and open trial. If, on the other hand, his only guilt has been rebellion, let a great nation show the truest quality of greatness—magnanimity—by including him in the wide folds of that act of amnesty and oblivion, in which all his minor partners, civil and military, in the late Confederacy are now so wisely enveloped. Make him a martyr and his memory is dangerous; treat him with the generosity of liberation, and he both can and, we think, will be a power for good in the future of peace and restored prosperity which we hope for the Southern States.

Believing that the views of Mr. Davis may throw important light on the true policy to be pursued, the author noted down all such as he could remember, or has had made notes of, as faithfully and as conscientiously as if giving his evidence under oath in a court of justice. Nowhere has he sought to better by concealment or misrepresentation the actual character or views of the person for whom he confesses that his professional, and finally his personal sympathies, have been warmly enlisted; and the only points he has been led to suppress—and they have been very few—were such merely medical details as neither the public would care for, nor any physician be authorized to expose. "Be just even to your enemies," is not only one of the noblest, but wisest maxims which antiquity has left us; and there is another like unto it: "It is lawful, even from your enemies, to learn wisdom."

And now with some few suggestive questions, this final chapter will be brought to a close.

Has any evidence yet been brought before the Reconstruction Committee of our Congress been franker, clearer, more evidently honest, or more heartily aiming to bring before the country the actual needs, wishes, and aspirations of the South than that of such gentlemen as Robert E. Lee, Alexander H. Stephens, and the other late leaders of the rebellion, who have been examined, and whose testimony has been spread before the public? And has there not been manifest in all such testimony yet taken, an unreserved acquiescence in the results of the recent war, and a very earnest desire to restore the relations of the Union on a basis of harmony, good faith, and future complete assimilation of interests and institutions which shall endure for ever? The intelligent of the beaten rebels are to-day, and likely to remain, as faithful supporters of the Union as can be found on the face of the globe—is not this conceded? And while the opinions of the gentlemen examined have been regarded and treated by the highest authority as of deserved importance in aiding us to solve the problem of reconstruction—can it be wise, we ask, that those of Mr. Davis, their confessedly ablest leader in the political field, and the man most powerful over the affections and confidence of the Southern masses, should be now ignored in silence, or for ever suppressed in the silent cell of an untried and unconvicted imprisonment? For the crime of treason, not one of these—not the humblest official under the late rebellion—was one whit more or less guilty than the man whom they elected their titular President; and if any other crimes can be alleged against him, in the name of justice, and for the honor of our whole country, both now and in the hereafter, are not his friends and suffering family entitled to demand that he may have an early and impartial trial as provided by the laws of our country?

THE END.